Dating and Mating in a Techno-Driven World

DATING AND MATING IN A TECHNO-DRIVEN WORLD

Understanding How Technology Is Helping and Hurting Relationships

Rachel Hoffman

Sex, Love, and Psychology
Judy Kuriansky, Series Editor

 PRAEGER™

An Imprint of ABC-CLIO, LLC
Santa Barbara, California • Denver, Colorado

Copyright © 2018 by Rachel Hoffman

Library of Congress Cataloging in Publication Control Number: 2017045938

ISBN: 978-1-4408-5732-4 (print)
        978-1-4408-5733-1 (ebook)

22 21 20 19 18   1 2 3 4 5

This book is also available as an eBook.

Praeger
An Imprint of ABC-CLIO, LLC

ABC-CLIO, LLC
130 Cremona Drive, P.O. Box 1911
Santa Barbara, California 93116-1911
www.abc-clio.com

This book is printed on acid-free paper ∞

Manufactured in the United States of America

This book is dedicated to my Grandpa Mel Z"L, who

always inspired me to dream

bigger, to work harder, and to never settle. I know he

would be proud but I wish I

could see his reaction to me becoming an author.

CONTENTS

SERIES FOREWORD

Emojis. Swiping. Teledildonics. Ghosting and cushioning.

These are terms from technology that are impacting the sex and love lives of our clients and people of all ages today. As therapists and as members of the public, we need to be alert to such wordings, tools of technology, and treatment techniques to cope, which are crucial to our professional practice and personal relationships.

Rachel Hoffman is doing just that in this book. That is why I was thrilled to engage her to write about this topic for this Praeger series. As an early career psychologist, she is up-to-date on what's happening in the real world and applies that to our professional world. That is of value to all of us as sexuality and relationship professionals, as well as to experts from other fields and members of the general public.

We may know Skype, but do we know about autoanswering on Skype? Or about sexting on the cloud? Or about how Snapchat in being used in sex?

I certainly remember the beginning explosion of technology in the 1990s, when e-mailing emerged, and when radio was all the rage for call-in sexuality and love advice—as I did for decades on my popular *Love Phones* show that I documented in *Generation Sex* and that evolved quickly into online dating that I discussed in *The Complete Idiots Guide to Dating*, and when new tech-sex innovations developed that Dr. Elizabeth Schroeder and I included in many chapters in the valuable Praeger series, "Sex Education: Past, Present and Future." More of those "future" applications pervasive now are presented importantly in this book.

This book's material is well organized and accessible—even fun—reading, besides being impressively backed up with academic research. One of my favorites is an explanation of sextexting addiction on the basis of reinforcement schedules from experimental psychology, notably, that unpredictable rewards cause greater increases of dopamine. Others of my favorites in this book are classic lessons I use in my classes about intimacy at Columbia University Teachers College, about the importance of "active listening," and also about attachment styles.

Chapters are well organized into four general elements: case narratives followed by relationship dynamic analysis, treatment techniques (for therapists but that can also be applied by general readers), and a summary of essential takeaways. Issues like emotional affairs and cyber-infidelity, as well as coping and therapeutic techniques from various disciplines, including cognitive behavioral therapy, emotionally focused therapy, and dialectical behavioral therapy, are addressed.

Rachel Hoffman certainly achieves her goal in this book: to mindfully control technology—instead of letting it control us—for better connections and closeness in sexuality and love.

Dr. Judy Kuriansky

PREFACE

This book was a project that began when I noticed a trend occurring with my clients. However, my passion for this topic began while analyzing tumultuous, exhilarating, serious, and casual relationships during high school through college. Relationships are complicated and may feel like an emotional roller coaster. You can have brief (or longer) periods of bliss, but at some point, you will have to deal with the challenges that step into your path. Through my personal and professional experience, I have seen couples tackle a range of difficulties, some more challenging than others. Affairs, lack of intimacy, inadequate communication, and opposing parenting styles are just a few of the stumbling blocks couples may face. Technology presents another potential obstacle, which can damage relationships. However, commitment and dedication can repair that damage.

Technology can also be an asset to your relationship if used properly. Utilizing "airplane mode" made a big difference in improving intimacy in my own relationship. Having respect for yourself, as well as your partner, is a pillar of a successful relationship. Striving for personal growth and relationship development is difficult but rewarding. The act of making behavioral changes to improve intimacy is a symbol of dedication and commitment. Ultimately, I am hoping to provoke an "Aha" moment where you reassess your use of technology.

ACKNOWLEDGMENTS

Thank you to Kayla Brock, an incredible intern and researcher. Tammy Nelson, I appreciate you as an unbelievable mentor, teacher, and leader in the field. I am fortunate to have worked with Inara de Luna, editor extraordinaire and Chicago style expert!

Lastly, I want to thank my friends and family for their support. Sigal, thanks for your comedic relief and creative inspiration. Avi, Oren, and Ari, thank you for your insight and special skillsets. Mom, I think you deserve more than a shout-out in this book. I will treat you to a long massage. Dad, thank you also for being inquisitive and for always being my biggest fan. To my friends, I know I have not been as available and fun this past year, so thank you for continuing to check in to make sure I am alive.

Chapter 1

INTRODUCTION

I want to take this opportunity to thank you for buying and reading my book. However, if you just use it as a coffee table book, I will let it slide. It is most important to me, however, that you have a clear understanding of my mission for this book and what I hope it accomplishes. If one piece of advice or analysis of a trend gives you a different perspective of yourself and of your relationships, then I have succeeded.

I was amazed at how often technology played a significant role in the relationship and dating issues experienced by my clients. People who come for therapy experience a wide variety of problems and/or symptoms. However, I often discovered (sometimes only after multiple sessions) some form of technology played a key role in their relationship struggles. For example, some individuals in relationships were unable to part from their phones, causing tension and distance between partners. Many of my clients were also in the casual dating stage, struggling with the confusion and anxiety of modern courtship. The invention of online dating has many benefits, in that it provides alternative ways to meet and network. However, the excess of choices introduces new complications and stressors.

As I watched this theme emerge repeatedly, I highlighted and analyzed certain trends. I subsequently realized that all clinicians need to be aware of this phenomenon. As our society evolves and technology further develops, relationship dynamics will continue to shift and we will have to adapt accordingly. Therefore, the types of issues affecting relationships will also change, and treatment techniques will have to be modified. Cognitive behavioral therapy, emotionally focused therapy, and dialectical behavioral therapy are just some of the methods that can be tailored for the treatment of technology-related issues. I sought ways to use these already-established practices in working with the couples and individuals you will meet in this book.

My goal is for individuals who are currently dating or in relationships to take a step back and look at their own behaviors as well as the behaviors of their partners. However, I do not just mean think about it for a few seconds. I mean look at yourself and your relationships critically. This book should ultimately encourage mindfulness. I want you, the reader, to observe yourself from an outside perspective and think how, why, and when you utilize technology. What types of feelings emerge when you scroll social media or observe a partner preoccupied on his or her phone? My hope is that you finish reading this book and take concrete action steps to feel lighter, freer, and less dependent on technology.

Reading Aziz Ansari's book, *Modern Romance*, was enlightening and inspiring. He did a phenomenal job of outlining the key components of contemporary relationships and presenting studies that explain the phenomenon. He was also hilarious, which made writing this book certainly challenging. Although I am not necessarily trying to be comedic, I would appreciate a few laughs here and there. I hope to be informative as well as engaging. His book introduced and explained modern romance, and I will highlight a few of those trends with applicable treatment strategies.[1]

The structure of the book is as follows: I begin each chapter with a case study or narrative. Most of the case studies are based on clients that I have seen personally or were described anonymously by peers. Other narratives are from friends of mine who were willing to share their experiences. I want to thank these individuals for being vulnerable in disclosing their personal stories. All the names and personally identifying information of these individuals and couples have been changed for confidentiality.

After presenting the case study or narrative, I analyze the relationship dynamic, looking into the psychology behind the problem. I present thought-provoking research that speaks to the specific trends in each chapter. Treatment techniques will then be offered for therapists to use; however, if you are dating or in a relationship, you will certainly be able to apply some of the tools provided. Lastly, a summary of the chapter will leave you with the most essential takeaways. The chapter headings are organized so that it is possible to skip or skim over parts that you personally find less relevant and still get much out of the chapter.

One chapter is outlined differently. In the chapter on dating apps, I share about the qualitative study I conducted, in which I interviewed individuals and focus groups about their experiences using the different apps. Therefore, I especially want to thank all those individuals who gave me diverse perspectives and shared with me their experiences and emotions regarding this topic. Their names were also changed to protect their privacy.

You might feel that the chapter headings are random, and that there are many more topics within the field of technology and dating. You would be justified! It is simply not feasible to consider all the related facets of this constantly evolving topic. It is equally difficult to keep up with all the new products and applications that are developed. The goal here was not just to illuminate the issues, but to provide realistic expectations and share reasonable tools you can use on a daily basis to improve your life and relationships. It is likely that at least one chapter in this book will make you stop and think, "Wow, this resembles or parallels my life." If that happens, then I have reached my objective.

I am not just writing as a therapist, but as a 27-year-old female who has personally experienced the effect that technology has on relationships. It can create tension and anxiety when partners are more in touch with their devices than each other. Having shared experiences and stimulating conversations are necessary for relationship growth. The possibility to connect with one another is so much more feasible when you sometimes remove those external distractions. The act of removing technology from a room symbolizes your level of interest and consideration for the person or people around you. Alternatively, staring at your phone and/or computer sends a clear message of your priorities.

However, I am also aware that technology is necessary and can even have positive and beneficial impacts on relationships. Sharing hilarious YouTube videos, sexting, and using teledildonics are just some of the incredible ways to incorporate technology into a relationship.

It is also important to remember the reality that we live in a world where work does not necessarily end when you leave the office. The competitive nature of modern society instills a need to be *more* connected than your coworker in order to achieve ultimate success. Therefore, when you step into your home, it is possible your work follows you and supersedes your relationship. This might be your reality. If this is the case, different types of modifications can accomplish similar goals dependent on your life situation. This does not mean that the change is any less significant.

It is important to note the case studies and therapeutic techniques introduced in this book can benefit all types of relationships, regardless of sexual orientation or gender identity. Although the techniques offered for treatment are based on the specific case scenarios, they can easily be generalized. My hope is that they can be applicable in some way for your own relationship or dating experience.

Additionally, I attempt to explore the biology and psychology behind some of the actions taken by both men and women. I want to be clear that both genders can ghost, get distracted by technology, cheat, and have phone addictions. This book is not directed toward either gender or meant to offend either gender. I provide potential explanations for certain behaviors and tools for therapists to assist with those behaviors. Regardless of whether you opt for monogamy, polyamory, or another type of relationship, these strategies can be applied.

Why is it so necessary to write an entire book about technology and relationships? Well, technology and relationships are both worldly constructs that people value tremendously. Roughly three-quarters of Americans (77%) now own a smartphone.[2] Nearly seven in ten Americans now use social media. This clearly affects the way we relate and connect to one another. The share of 18- to 24-year-olds who use online dating has roughly tripled from 10 percent in 2013 to 27 percent today (2017).[3] Fifty percent of teens have let someone know they were interested in them romantically by friending them on Facebook or another social media site.[4] The way humans connect and interact is shifting. Children are receiving smartphones, iPads, and tablets at earlier ages. College students are beginning to utilize dating apps to "hook up." We all need to be prepared to address how this affects us as individuals and as a society.

Work is already being done to address these growing trends. According to researcher Katherine Hertlein, "While there are certainly negative impacts of technology in couple relationships, advanced technology also can have a positive impact on couples and families."[5] Her goal was to integrate the use of technology positively within the intersystems approach for the treatment of sexual dysfunction. She discusses the sociocultural factors related to technology that can affect intimacy in a relationship. She said, "Many individuals hold jobs that are greatly facilitated by increased usage of technology, including being able to check e-mail from home, receiving phone calls from employers and coworkers while at home, and increased opportunities to work from home. This can blur the lines between home and work life and result in reduced intimacy between partners."[6]

Hertlein's summary offers future directions for researchers and clinicians. As technological advances continue to develop, couple and family therapists will be faced with more challenges related to technology and their lives. She stated, "Therapists need to continue to develop strategies to address the influence of technology in people's lives as well as identifying ways to use the technology to improve interpersonal relationships."[7] That is exactly what I set out to do in my professional career and I relay my findings in this book.

There is undeniably more work to be done. As technology develops further and virtual reality becomes a norm for interacting, researchers will need to continue studying the implications on dating and relationships. Therapists will also have to shift their treatment methods to address the various forms of meeting and courting, as well as the range of issues that arise from the impact of technology on the relationship.

My overall professional goal is to enhance relationships and to improve modern dating. If you are more self-aware of your intentions and goals of dating, then you are more likely to achieve success in your relationships. In addition to reflecting on your use of technology, the practice of mindfulness can spread into other facets of your life. Being aware of your behaviors, and the intentions behind your actions, can help create a much healthier lifestyle.

Enjoy reading, and I hope you gain some guidance on how to navigate this complex world of technology, dating, and relationships.

Chapter 2

WHY WON'T HE TEXT ME?

CASE STUDY: JULIE'S POST-DATE STRESS

Mark, a 27-year-old heterosexual male, and Julie, a 28-year-old heterosexual female, were set up through a mutual friend. Their first date was at a casual bar in the lower east side of downtown Manhattan. Julie was nervous. She spent hours picking out her outfit and decided on high-waisted jeans and a black tank top. She became anxious as her mind filled with questions. Would she recognize Mark? Would they have common interests? Sufficient topics of conversation? Or would there be long pauses of awkward silence? After an extensive pep talk from her best friend, Samantha, she felt prepared and confident.

Afterward, Julie thought the date went smoothly. They discussed their love for travel, specifically in South America. Mark laughed when Julie told the story about her freshman-year roommate, who woke up to an alarm clock blasting Broadway show tunes. They both were close to their families and loved the excitement of a football tailgate. Overall, Julie felt an emotional connection. She called Samantha.

"Sam, that was the best date. He was attentive and sweet. We had so much in common. It felt great." Julie went to sleep with a smile on her face. The next day she couldn't focus at work. She told her coworkers all about the date and wondered aloud when she would hear from him.

"He'll definitely text you," her coworkers assured her. Three days passed, and Julie still hadn't heard a word from Mark. Cue the next call to Samantha.

"Sam. I am freaking out. *Why won't he text me*!?"

ANALYSIS: WHY DO WOMEN WAIT?

Sound familiar? How many times have you heard a friend utter these painful words "Why won't he text me?" How many times have you sat on the couch with your phone on your lap waiting for it to vibrate? You casually pick it up, turn it over, throw it on the bed, peek at it for a few seconds, throw it back on the bed, and pace around your room like a madwoman on speed. You can't resist checking your phone 30 times a minute and then suddenly the feelings of despair, frustration, and confusion emerge. You wonder what weird thing you said or did on your last date. Where did it go wrong? Did you laugh awkwardly? Talk too much about your family? Open up too soon about your previous relationship?

Julie's escalating insecurity about not hearing from her date was an understandable progression. She assumed that due to the strong chemistry on their date, Mark would be itching to text her and to see her again. After all, her *perception* was that they had a great first date where the conversation flowed naturally. She felt hopeful to have finally met someone, after so many unbearable dates, who shared similar goals, interests, and values. Naturally, she believed she would hear from him again and felt disappointed when she did not receive a follow-up text.

THERAPY: INTERPRETING THE TEXTING AMBIGUITY

Julie presented to therapy exhausted, with the goal of gaining a better understanding of her dating failures. After validating and empathizing with her feeling of disappointment, we worked on assessing her needs and desires in a partner. During one of Julie's sessions, I questioned why *she* waited to hear from *him*. It seemed, from Julie's description, that the success of the date would warrant a follow-up text regardless of who initiated. Although women have taken tremendous strides in certain areas of American culture, including the growth of women in professions traditionally dominated by men, many women continue to take a passive role when it comes to dating. In modern dating, the female continues to wait for a text as if the male is in complete control of her future. Julie was a valued leader at her place of employment. She was a supervisor of a team of 20 and confidently advocated for a promotion. However, when it came to the dating world, Julie took a backseat. Her confidence in herself dwindled, and her feelings of loneliness became more apparent. Attitudes toward gender roles have continued to evolve since women achieved the right to vote in 1920. I hypothesize that behavior takes longer than attitude to transform. Each new generation will benefit from the actions of their role models. Julie, who herself was well educated and experienced, had a mom who worked out of the home. However, her background also reinforced more traditional male/female roles when it came to relationships.

Julie explained during her session that receiving a text from Mark would validate the connection that she felt during the date. That text would prove his interest and provide her with the confidence and encouragement to move forward. It was like a game of chess, where she was static until he made his move.

While working with Julie on becoming more self-aware of her desires in a partner, we explored the fact that she was waiting for a text message as opposed to a phone call. I often discuss this common phenomenon of modern dating with my clients between the ages of 20 and 30. I have asked a number of them how they would feel about calling someone they were casually dating. Their response was mostly laughter, or they commented, "That's weird," or "I'd be uncomfortable." This was vastly different from the responses of my clients over the age of 40, who almost always called people they were casually dating.

It was interesting for me to explore with Julie, as well as with other clients, from where this phone discomfort stemmed, as many of my clients already interacted with a "partner" face-to-face. *Many of them kissed at the end of the night.* They literally shared saliva with another human being but were terrified to hear their date's voice.

Julie strongly preferred texts to calls, which is completely understandable. There is no immediate harm in favoring texts to calls. It was more important for Julie to be self-aware of her predilection. This tends to be my sentiment when working with my clients navigating the dating world: *Be aware of whichever method you prefer.* Are you someone who wants that quick check-in phone call mid-day? Would you rather have a good morning text or a good morning chat and walk? Does hearing your partner's voice provide you with comfort before bed, or does a simple "sleep well" text do the trick? You might also change your mind over the course of dating, which is fine as well. Self-awareness and communication go a long way, even if it is about the simplistic nature of texting versus calling. Maybe this should be a new question on dating apps. (See Figure 2.1.)

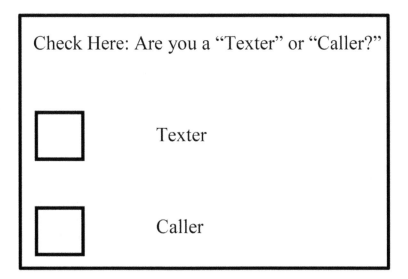

Figure 2.1 Communication Preference

ANALYSIS: A DOWNSIDE OF TEXTING IS LACK OF COMMUNICATION

As a society, we evolve and adapt to the changes in technology. Instead of meeting in person, we meet face-to-face in Skype or Google Hangout. Instead of going to a library, we search an online database. Naturally, dating patterns shift and modernize. Texting has become the new "normal" for scheduling dates. It can be both an impulsive and an immediate way to voice interest without bothering the person in that moment. The person is able to respond at a time suitable for him or her, which is beneficial when life is demanding. Texting also is helpful when in a public, loud space, where speaking aloud is frowned upon. Sounds great! So what is the problem?

Our ability to simply send a text instead of engaging in a genuine face-to-face conversation is one of the major contributors to Generation Y and the Millennial Generation's inability to start a relationship without the assistance of cell phones. Recently, researchers have been conducting studies to examine how technology is playing a role in forming and maintaining relationships. For example, Jessica Donn and Richard Sherman[1] conducted two studies to examine young adults' attitudes and practices about using the Internet to facilitate the formation of intimate relationships.

They found that graduate school students were more accepting than undergraduates about using the Internet as a resource for meeting people. Graduate students were not as likely to see forming relationships online as desperate and agreed more than undergraduates that there is nothing wrong with trying to meet people online. The researchers discussed possible reasons for these findings. One explanation was that graduate students are older and thus closer to the age at which many people marry. Therefore, they may have greater empathy for the desire to meet people. Another explanation was that graduate students may already be using the Internet for other purposes, in the form of professional networking or arranging meetings at conferences. This might lead to more comfort in using the Internet to form relationships. One other explanation is that graduate students have less free time, so they use the Internet as a time-management tool. Due to ease of use, the students utilized technology to form relationships. Many were frustrated with the stress of meeting people at bars, work, and events, and therefore embraced the novelty of online dating.

Nancy Baym, author of *Personal Connections in the Digital Age*, discusses why "we might like people we meet online more than those we meet offline."[2] She quotes Baker: "When we decide someone has appeals such as humor, good response time, or writing style, it is easy to fill in the blanks about their other traits with ideals."[3] Baym also notes that we have more control over our own responses. We can be more selective about what we reveal and when. Have you ever erased, rewrote, or deleted a text before sending? This is the premise to which she is referring. Baym also found that the more intimate the relationship of college students, the more likely they were to use face-to-face conversations and telephone calls. Most of their relationships began with texting, which allowed for increased control and allowed the other person to respond at a convenient time. The students also stated that "relational closeness can also be symbolized with Facebook wall posts or changing relationship status on Facebook."[4] If you aren't official on Facebook, you aren't really dating. Baym summarizes an article by Larson in which he identifies four types of courtship relationships: hanging out, just talking, dating, and hooking up.[5] Baym states, "As the courtship develops, moving to the telephone becomes a turning point symbolizing greater seriousness and commitment."[6] It is clear, based on Baym and Larson's research, that the method of communicating can signify the stage of the relationship, especially for college-age students. I hypothesize that when you are more committed and at a further along stage, you worry less about how your message comes across. Once you are more familiar with your partner's verbiage and feel confident about your partner's feelings toward the relationship, you worry less about the implications of your words. There is less of a concern that what you say will affect the outcome of the relationship.

ANALYSIS: AN UPSIDE OF TEXTING IS DECREASED ANXIETY

Although texting might be harmful in terms of developing communication skills, it also has some advantages. One benefit of texting is that it is shown to decrease anxiety. A study conducted by Amanda Klein revealed that "during the early stages of a relationship or in casual dating scenarios, texting is an ideal mode of communication as it helps reduce uncertainty and lessen anxiety. As participants noted, once a connection is established, additional forms of communication are introduced."[7]

Texting creates an emotional barrier between you and your partner. Reading is more of a passive experience than verbal communication. Instead of having to hear "no" or an excuse over the phone, one would rather read the words through a text message and quickly delete to avoid feeling rejected. In other words, it is a tangible defense mechanism.

Another benefit to texting is that you can distract yourself while waiting for an answer. You can shower, go to dinner, or watch a movie. Remember how often you send a text and then purposefully distract yourself to avoid checking for a response. Although you speculate the entire time if a reply has arrived and what it says, by avoiding it you can delay the possibility of feeling hurt. For Julie, the absence of a follow-up text was a blatant rejection. Her relationship with Mark did not progress far enough to enter the stage of texting back and forth, otherwise known as the casual dating period.

RESEARCH: GETTING HIGH OFF OF WAITING

During this casual dating period, there is a buildup of excitement. Think of that high you feel when you are waiting for that text back. Envision the giddiness and the intense emotion that circulate through your entire body and prevent you from keeping still. Why do you feel that way? The answer is the chemical dopamine. Dopamine is a neurotransmitter that controls the brain's reward and pleasure centers. Think of it as the "happy" chemical that is released in the brain, which makes you feel good, positive, and excited.[8]

One myth of dopamine is that it is released when you receive a reward. In actuality, the brain releases more dopamine in anticipation of that reward. Neuroscientist Robert Sapolsky conducted a study in which he trained monkeys to press a button after a light went on.[9] After the tenth time pressing a button, the monkeys received a food treat. Sapolsky measured the dopamine levels during this experiment. The levels were the highest during the signal/button phase. Sapolsky concluded that dopamine was released at a higher level when there was unpredictability and anticipation.

Unpredictability increases anticipatory anxiety—when the monkeys got the treat all the time, a fair amount of dopamine was released during the pressing phase. When getting the treat was unpredictable, the amount of dopamine went up. So what does this behavior teach us about dating? Waiting for a text back increases that nervous anticipation. What is he going to say? What is he thinking? That dopamine release is addicting, so in a sense, the texting and waiting becomes an addictive process.

In experimental psychology, the theory of reinforcement involves fixed versus variable reward schedules. Fixed refers to when the number of responses between reinforcements, or the amount of time between reinforcements, is set and unchanging. Variable refers to when the number of responses or amount of time between reinforcements varies or changes. For example, a fixed reward is when you get paid on a regular cycle. You work a certain amount of hours a week and then, either biweekly or weekly, you get the same paycheck. A variable reward can be compared to gambling. You can play and play for hours or a minute, and the amount of money you win can vary widely and is unrelated to how long you gambled. It is clear that gambling can become addictive. Again, the reason is that *unpredictable rewards cause greater increases in the level of dopamine*. Therefore, either not receiving a text back or having to wait an unpredictable amount of time can increase dopamine levels. It is truly fascinating how our minds work. Something that seems so inherently painful and anxiety provoking can produce mental rushes and thrills that keep us craving more.

CASE STUDY: MOLLY'S TEXTING DEBACLES

Molly is a 27-year-old heterosexual woman navigating the dating world. She utilizes multiple dating apps and is determined to find a partner. She feels extremely frustrated by the texts she receives after first dates. The texts confuse and anger her to the point she feels like giving up. Here are a couple examples of texts she received after first dates:

Conversation #1:	Steve
Steve:	Hey what's going on?
Molly:	Nothing much just got home from work u?
Steve:	Niceee (*notice multiple "eee"s*). Just chillen. Any plans this weekend?
Molly:	Not really, prob going out. U?
Steve:	Cool, same. Hopefully I'll see you!

ANALYSIS: AMBIGUOUS MOTIVATIONS

Molly panics. She immediately sends her friend the screenshot of the conversation. Her friend calls her, and they enter the analyzing stage. "He 'hopes' he wants to see me? If he wants to see me, why doesn't he just ask me out? Is this a booty call? Should I ignore his last text?"

A telephone call, in this situation, would remove the ambiguity. The phone call itself would express his sincerity. The tone of his voice would reemphasize his genuineness. Lastly, they would inevitably hang up with an already-made plan. Ultimately, the point is that texting is limiting. All you have is the few words in front of you and your brain attempting to decipher the meaning and implications of those words.

Conversation #2:	Matt
Molly:	Hey Matt, how's your day going?
Matt:	Good, already thinking about the weekend haha
Molly:	haha same, what are you doing this weekend?
Matt:	not much, relaxing, going out, same old
Molly:	nice, same. We should hang out
Matt:	For sure

ANALYSIS: INDIRECTNESS LEADS TO UNCERTAINTY

This is the classic "we should hang out" message. In all forms of communication, when one utilizes slang or other common-use phrases, it allows the other to proscribe meaning. Texting is a platform that encourages shortcuts.

Between friends, these shortcuts greatly simplify communication. However, people sometimes forget that with these timesavers, as with all slang, they carry multiple meanings and can easily be misconstrued. In these situations, it might be best to insist on clarity to avoid anxiety and uncertainty.

These conversations are frustrating for individuals because so many times they end up with no hangout, just overthinking and overanalyzing. With no plan solidified, there is more waiting and speculating. Matt's intention is unclear. I can speculate that he has no interest in seeing Molly, as he did not persist in creating a plan. On the other hand, perhaps he is unsure of his plans, wants to see if something more enticing presents itself, and if not, he has Molly as a secure and fun backup. Regardless, Molly certainly wants to see Matt and feels annoyed at this outcome. Although she initiated the text, clearly steering him in the direction to ask her out, he failed to take the bait. Molly, at this point, begins the waiting game to see if he "makes a move" over the weekend. Again, without Matt's tone voicing sincerity, the ambiguous text can leave much to the imagination.

CASE STUDY: PAM AND THE TEXTING GAME

When Pam, a 28-year-old heterosexual woman, came to see me for therapy, she told me she was "over dating" and proceeded to explain her latest experience. She went on two dates with a guy named Matt, also 28, and felt that they had a "great connection." Although he was consistent with his texting, he did not ask her out for a third date. The texts mostly consisted of casual banter about food and television shows.

One night at 11 p.m., after she attended a concert with a friend, he texted her to come over. She replied, "I'm not really that type of girl. If you want to see me, you know what to do." He responded, "I miss your face." Pam was frustrated. She decided to ignore his last text, hoping he would get the message that she wanted another date, but instead, the next day he followed up with more small talk in texts. Pam's frustration turned into anger, which she acknowledged in therapy.

ANALYSIS: THE TEXTING GAME

What is the texting game? This approach involves playing mind games with your partner, creating the illusion that you are "hard to get," confident, and independent. According to Helen Fisher, "Games are the way we keep romance alive. They're based in human hardwiring. Playing hard-to-get or leaving a little to the imagination allows the woman to be wooed and appreciated and the man to be challenged and intrigued."[10]

The game can be used in all types of relationships. Neil Strauss, author of *Rules of the Game*, created a 30-day challenge where he guaranteed that after completion, a man will solidify a date with a woman. He claimed that he spent "five years gathering this knowledge, living it, and sharing it . . . and the result is a month-long workout program for your social, attraction, dating, and seduction skills."[11] He claims that his challenge helps build confidence and knowledge to meet and attract almost any woman at any time.

Playing "the game" takes effort and energy, and can be exhausting. It can also be confusing, overwhelming, and draining. Pam's experience was an example of this phenomenon.

THERAPY: THE TEXTING DEFENSE

Pam came to therapy to analyze her dating experiences. I explained to Pam that she and Matt both utilized texts as a barrier to protect themselves from exploring and expressing deeper emotions or intentions. Pam's response to Matt's text symbolized a distorted, false sense of confidence. She felt anger and confusion, yet instead of outwardly stating her feelings and her desire for another date, she continued with the texting "game." Despite his random, somewhat obnoxious text about her face, she was still hoping that if she ignored his 11 p.m. text, there would be an opportunity to take this relationship further. Her "misreading" in the moment allowed for defensive denial. Matt kept the banter going, presumably to entice Pam to sleep with him, or perhaps he was unsure what he wanted. However, after Pam ignored his final message, Matt pursued Pam with meaningless texts, further contributing to Pam's confusion and insecurity. Both parties hid their true desires by playing these "games."

I asked Pam about her ideal scenario with dating. After a long pause, she stated, "Ideally, I would love if we made consistent plans, perhaps twice a week, and had a few daily texts back and forth throughout the dating process." I probed further, asking her what the consistent plans and daily texts meant to her. She explained that the consistency provided her with security— security that they were moving in the right direction and security that he was interested. We determined together that Matt was not meeting Pam's needs. Although they did have casual banter regularly, he did not fulfill her need of securing weekly plans. After we made this conclusion, I asked her why she continued with the "texting game." She thought briefly and then stated, "I felt like I could almost trick or convince him into asking me out. I thought that if I got him to ask me, we would have a really good time and then he would want me more." This was Pam demonstrating great self-awareness and insight. However, did Pam really want a relationship to begin with "tricking" her partner to ask her out? We further explored in this session that, to Pam, having meaningful, regular dates indicates a sign of respect. Therefore, engaging in the texting game with Matt was a symptom of Pam's own insecurities.

THERAPY: THE ROLE OF LOW SELF-ESTEEM IN TEXTING

Over time, we explored Pam's diminished self-esteem and how it enabled her to participate in aimless relationships. One of Pam's goals was to increase her confidence to understand the type of relationship she yearned for and deserved. Embarking in the dating world will inevitably lead to rejection and uncomfortable situations. Having self-confidence would provide Pam with the skills, tools, and language to state her desire, needs, and goals for the relationship.

Part of Pam's fear was coming across as "crazy," common for many of my female clients navigating the dating world. We delved deep into this fear in therapy. Was her priority to lose herself in an effort to attract a man or would she rather walk away with her integrity?

Pam's mind-set of attempting to gain control of the relationship was one that many individuals express when presenting to therapy. In an effort to appear confident and at ease, they portray themselves in a specific way through technology. They aim to appear independent and unemotional. Therefore, instead of expressing their needs in a straightforward fashion, they are indirect and passive. Both men and women are guilty of beating around the bush; however, this only creates a world of confusion, misunderstandings, and a lack of connection. It is the responsibility of both parties to be transparent. If you are unable to be yourself, have increased anxiety from the relationship, or feel insecure about expressing your needs, it is perhaps not the right emotional or romantic fit. Therapy helped Pam recognize this trend and gave her the space to practice being more open and self-aware. She ultimately decided that being blunt and straightforward led to better results and greater self-respect. She discontinued her trend of "casually chatting" with men if no dates were scheduled. Pam remained committed to her values, which in turn gave her more confidence and led to better results in the dating world.

RESEARCH: PSYCHOLOGICAL EXPLANATIONS OF TEXTING

The question posed at the beginning of this chapter was "Why won't he text me?" It is impossible to know the exact answer without asking the person in question. However, there are certainly possible *psychological* explanations.

1. *His brain is wired that way.* Male brains utilize nearly seven times more *gray matter* for activity, while female brains utilize nearly ten times more *white matter*. What does this mean? Gray matter areas of the brain are localized. According to Gregory Jantz, "They are information and action-processing centers in specific splotches in a specific area of the brain. This can translate to a kind of tunnel vision when they are doing something."[12] Once a person becomes deeply engaged in a task or game, he or she may not demonstrate

much sensitivity to other people or his or her surroundings. Males tend, after reflecting briefly on an emotive memory, to analyze it somewhat and then move onto the next task. During this process, they may also choose to change course and do something active and unrelated to feelings, rather than analyze their feelings at all. White matter is the networking grid that connects the brain's gray matter and other processing centers with one another. So I will explain in layman's terms. A woman might send a text hoping to elicit a response. She then sits with anxiety, waiting for a response (possibly attempting to distract herself). Even while working, hanging out with friends, or watching television, her brain is still sitting in that pool of anxiety. The man she texted received the text, acknowledged it, and then became distracted by his next activity. Again, this is a generalization and does not reflect the behavior of all males and females. This also works on a continuum, and you will sometimes find males encompassing traits that are typically described as feminine. For more information on this, you can read Robert Heasley's typology, *Queer Masculinities of Straight Men.*[13]

2. *He wants to be "less available."* Authors Aziz Ansari and Eric Klinenberg discuss the power of appearing scarce to make yourself seem more attractive. They present an idea from social psychology called the scarcity principle. "Basically, we see something as more desirable when it is less available. When you are texting someone less frequently, you are, in effect, creating a scarcity of *you* and making yourself more attractive."[14]

3. *Women sometimes want ambivalent partners.* Studies have proven women tend to desire men who are uncertain about their feelings toward them. Erin Whitchurch, Timothy Wilson, and Daniel Gilbert, researchers at the University of Virginia, conducted a study where women were shown Facebook profiles of men who they were told had viewed their profiles.[15] Ansari and Klinenberg summarize the research:

> One group was shown profiles of men who they were told had rated their profiles the best. A second group was told they were seeing profiles of men who had said their profiles were average. And a third group was shown profiles of men and told it was "uncertain" how much the men liked them. The women were *most* attracted to the "uncertain" group. They also later reported thinking about the "uncertain" men the most. When you think about people more, this increases their presence in your mind, which ultimately can lead to feelings of attraction.[16]

Therefore, not getting a text response might subconsciously lead you to think about your partner more. This is clearly frustrating because it would be simpler to prefer people who were clear and open about their feelings. Unfortunately, our brains are not exactly wired that way.

4. *He's just not interested.* In other words, the date did not go well, and he does not want to see you again and prefers to avoid confrontation of any sort.

TIP: RETHINKING REJECTION IN TEXTING

Pam labeled her feelings of vulnerability, disappointment, and sadness as rejection. This led to a downward spiral in which she felt personally attacked. She told herself that she had been rejected and that she wasn't "cool" enough, attractive enough, or smart enough to warrant a third date. Negative self-talk can be dangerous! Concentrating on rejection can preclude self-reflection. Until Pam was able to reflect on her own feelings toward Matt, she had a one-sided view of the encounter.

Matt's texting behavior appeared to reveal an attitude antithetical to Pam's goals. Pam's focus on the texts distracted her from the larger issue, that she and Matt were pursuing different types of relationship at this time. It hurt because she initially thought there was potential. She labeled the experience as rejection, which I helped her reframe as disappointment.

The dating process will inevitably include developing an understanding of the other's values, goals, and needs. To find a partner, whether casual or long term, you must first be self-aware. Dating will unfortunately entail uncomfortable experiences and meeting people who do not fit your criteria. Instead of feeling "rejected" when things do not go as planned, try to feel encouraged that you are putting yourself out there even if you have not yet found your match.

Another way to confront your anxiety or disappointment and to re-evaluate the "rejection" is to question your desires for this individual. Step away from the rejection and consider your date. Is this someone with whom you genuinely connected or were you more enamored with the idea of a relationship? An understandable, initial reaction to being rejected is to be hurt and maybe confused. However, if the dates were only "okay" and the conversation was meager, it might be better that the relationship ended sooner rather than later.

Feeling rejected may negatively influence one's sense of self-worth. To cope, it helps to first identify the feeling and the source. Give yourself a little time to feel and heal. Then do a self-check. Did you see any signs or have concerns about it ending? Have you been in similar situations? If you can learn from the experience, moving on comes more naturally. Remember, a rejection from someone who barely knows you is not a rejection of you. If the relationship did not progress, you probably have not met your match or the timing was not right. However, modifying negative thoughts is challenging. Talk your "rejection" out with a friend and analyze your own feelings. It might help you see things more clearly. Many of my clients admit to feeling superior at the beginning of the relationship. They believe they are "better catches" than their partners. However, as soon as they get "rejected," they feel distraught, as if they lost out on the most amazing relationship. Part of treatment is learning to recognize and revise this illogical thought process.

TIP: STRATEGY TO ADDRESS WAITING

I have encouraged many of my female friends and clients to be more proactive while in the beginning stages of dating. This can be stressful, challenging, and outside their comfort zone, but it can also be a powerful statement that instills confidence. An initial text stating that you enjoyed the date can be a great starting point to a conversation. Why subject yourself to the added stress of waiting and overthinking? If he is not interested, then who cares anyway? Find out and move on.

I am not encouraging you to text multiple times, which can appear overeager. However, one initial text to break the ice should not ultimately hurt your chances for a second or third date.

IMPLICATIONS FOR THERAPISTS: LOOKING AT ATTACHMENT

As a therapist, you will certainly have clients from all stages of the dating world present to your office. Clients of all ages may be confused as they attempt to interpret and analyze the behaviors of the individuals they date. Understanding why clients might feel anxious in relation to certain dating behaviors can be helpful for treatment.

Attachment theory, developed by John Bowlby, states that a strong emotional and physical attachment to at least one primary caregiver is critical to personal development. In the 1980s, Cindy Hazan and Phillip Shaver were two of the first researchers to explore Bowlby's ideas in the context of romantic relationships. Hazan and Shaver identified three types of insecure attachment: avoidant, ambivalent/anxious, and secure.[17]

- Avoidant: People with this attachment strategy are characterized as being afraid of intimacy, experiencing emotional highs and lows during relationships, along with much jealousy.

- Ambivalent/Anxious: People with this attachment style view love in an obsessive way, with a strong need for constant reciprocation and validation, along with emotional highs and lows, and feelings of jealousy and strong sexual attraction.

- Secure: Securely attached individuals describe their romantic relationships as friendly, trusting, and happy. They accept their partners regardless of faults. They tend to have long and fulfilling relationships.

An individual's level of attachment can strongly correlate with his or her need for validation in a relationship. Robert S. Weisskirch, a researcher and professor at California State University, conducted a study with female university students. The students were asked to estimate the frequency of calls and text messages sent and received from their romantic partners. Additionally, they completed the Experiences in Close Relationships-Revised instrument, a measurement of attachment anxiety and avoidance. According to Weisskirch:

> Individuals who have an anxious attachment are said to worry about their relationship, seek out reassurance, and pursue self-disclosure from their partners. In contrast, those who have an avoidant attachment are said to want to remain distant and maintain independence within a relationship. These attachment behavior patterns in relationships are likely to carry over to cell-phone communication. Text messaging may be a preferred kind of communication for those with anxious attachment because text messages are brief, textual reminders of the relational connection that also remains in the cell phone's memory and could serve as a visual representation of the relationship. Initiating text messages may also solicit a response, which may provide further reassurance.[18]

Weisskirch found that attachment avoidance was related to fewer estimated and actual calls made to the romantic partner. The implication of this study is that those individuals with anxious attachment personality types are more likely to need validation from a text message. They need more consistent ego stroking and reassurance.

Therapists have the tools to analyze the root of the anxiety in relation to texting. They can discuss family and romantic relationships with their clients, assessing for attachment or avoidance. Questions to explore familial relationships can assist in determining levels of attachments. Examples of questions include, "What role model did you have for relationships?" or "Describe your social life in school." After rapport has been established with clients, the therapist can openly share the connection between attachment and anxiety, and how it relates to texting in relationships. That connection will assist the client in understanding his or her behavior and the need to feel validated. It will set the stage for treatment.

IMPLICATIONS FOR THERAPY: OUTLINING GOALS AND EXPECTATIONS

Pam responded to this experience by making it an opportunity to explore her requirements. She identified and prioritized her convictions, values, and ideals. She became clearer as to what she wanted in a partner without making her desires so specific that they would be impossible to fulfill. This process required looking at family history and role models, as well as visualizing her future. Once she gained insight into her thought process in choosing a partner, she felt more prepared to restart the dating process.

Motivational interviewing is a great way to help clients determine their preferences in relationships. The goal is to guide clients to elicit self-realization in order to learn which behaviors are ego dystonic and ego syntonic. This will help create positive behavioral and relational changes while elucidating discrepancies between their thoughts and actions.

SUMMARY

Texting creates a new format for hurt and is a form of communication that can easily be misconstrued. Tones, nuances, and slang definitions are inferred by the reader. When clients present being obsessive about a text, I sometimes have them read it to me with different intonations. This enables them to see that they are projecting their feelings and thoughts into the words. For frequent texters, this is a strategy they could do on their own. It forces increased consciousness as to how one's own words, as well as those of others, can be misinterpreted.

In conclusion, therapists need to be familiar with how their clients use texting. This platform potentially increases regular communication between people who previously may not have connected during the day, albeit in short phrases and slang. This can positively enrich a relationship, especially when both parties are unable to have substantial interchanges during the day. However, because words are read and not spoken, it can easily lead to confusion and distress. This is especially true when the texters do not know each other's jargon well enough to accurately discern meaning. Being more mindful of how to utilize texting increases clarity and reduces subsequent anxiety.

Chapter 3

CAN YOU PUT DOWN YOUR PHONE, PLEASE?

CASE STUDY: PETE AND JOE'S WORK–LIFE BALANCE

Pete, a 33-year-old homosexual male, and Joe, a 37-year-old homosexual male, have been dating for six years and currently live together. They presented for therapy because they hadn't had sex in over two months. Pete, a corporate lawyer, often works until 11 p.m., while Joe, an elementary school teacher, is home by 4:30 p.m. After their joint session, I met with both Pete and Joe individually. Joe described how their relationship began with excitement and many shared experiences. They loved traveling and attending concerts. They considered themselves Billy Joel groupies. Once Pete began law school, he was consumed by schoolwork and networking. After school ended, Pete started working long hours at a corporate law firm. When he did get home and joined Joe in bed, he would skim his phone for e-mails and respond to texts he received throughout the day. Additionally, when they went out to dinner, Pete would keep his phone on the table. Every few minutes, his phone would vibrate with an e-mail from work.

Joe felt ignored and insignificant. When he would try to express this to Pete, Pete became defensive and explained that he was doing his best to balance work and the relationship, but it proved to be more difficult than he expected. Both Pete and Joe were committed to the relationship, but felt that the tension between them was becoming burdensome. Although the lack of sex was a trigger for them to begin therapy, they acknowledged there were underlying issues that needed to be addressed.

ANALYSIS: LIFE TRANSITIONS

Pete and Joe enjoyed the honeymoon stage of their relationship. The courting process included luxurious trips and exhilarating shared experiences that increased their emotional connection. However, once Pete began law school to further his career, the relationship dynamic shifted. They had to adjust to the limited time spent together. They did not prepare themselves for the transition. They were not prepared to compensate for Pete's long hours at work. They were not prepared for the lack of emotional and physical intimacy. Before they had time to fully process the transition, the distance between them became unbearable. They both felt hopeless, unsure how to balance the relationship with their personal needs and goals. When life becomes overwhelming, we tend to spend more time focusing on our devices. Our to-do list, calendars, contacts, messages, e-mails, and sources of entertainment are all located on our phones. Pete felt drawn to his phone and felt that drive to frequently check it for all work and personal matters.

ANALYSIS: FINDING THE WORK–LIFE BALANCE

For Pete and Joe, it was essential to acknowledge the impact that technology was having on their relationship. Most of us can empathize with the struggle of work–life balance. Due to an overwhelming drive to succeed and the competitive nature of some professions, accessibility becomes paramount. Not only do we plug in our phones and leave them on our night tables, how often do our laptops make the threesome? This drive to exceed expectations leads to the excessive checking of e-mails and "googling" articles from bed. The ruthless, tedious sequence of events proceeds like this: thoughts of creative ideas, preparations for the next day, financial worries, and relationship stressors consume our brain. Before settling on a specific thought, our fingers find themselves moving swiftly across the phone. Without a second of hesitation, we find ourselves scrolling *Business Insider*, *Elite Daily*, and Facebook. Multitasking has taken on a completely new dimension. Easy access to various types of information enables us to watch a funny video of a puppy going down a slide, followed immediately by a horrific chemical attack in Syria. I often wonder about what this does to us emotionally. Our smile remains from the puppy video, while feelings of shock erupt in response to the abomination of such an attack. Do we go back and return to the puppy? In addition to this emotional roller coaster, we are in the room with our partner, who may also be involved with their own device. However, it is also possible that your partner is sitting there needing to share with and receive from you. Now on your emotional plate, the puppy, the genocide, and your partner are all competing for a limited amount of emotional energy.

This leaves one partner feeling neglected, longing for his or her partner's attention. Meanwhile, the other person may be feeling drained and not quite sure why the partner feels so neglected. Is what they have to give so inadequate?

THERAPY: EXPECTATIONS AND NEEDS

Identifying the impact technology was having on Pete and Joe's relationship was a process that materialized over the course of multiple sessions. I discerned which of the behaviors were defensive/avoidant as opposed to more habitual. Working with Pete and Joe involved exploring the foundation of the relationship along with the needs of each partner. Joe felt disregarded and detached from Pete. His expectation was that the initial relationship, consisting of quality time, travel, and entertainment, would remain an essential part of their relationship. When technology disrupted their ability to connect emotionally, Joe withdrew. He did not want to put more energy into the relationship while simultaneously feeling dismissed.

Pete felt that the expectations set for him in all areas of his life were difficult to meet. His personal struggle with perfectionism, performance, and expectations were being acted out with work. He felt that he was always on call for his job and for his personal life. He knew how to succeed at his job, yet he felt that he could never satiate the needs of his partner. Technology, to Pete, was a necessity to thrive. He thought that Joe should be more understanding and proud that he was accomplishing his dreams. At the time he presented to therapy, he felt frustrated that no matter how hard he worked, he could not find a sense of peace in his life.

ANALYSIS: UNDERSTANDING ACTIVE LISTENING

Although many people have become phenomenal multitaskers, focusing on your partner while texting, scrolling, and responding is just not possible. We are not superhumans. I have seen relationships self-destruct as one partner appears semi-engaged in the life of his or her partner. Having technology as a presence in the room generates this feeling that *there is always something happening*. In order to avoid feeling behind or left out, you can alleviate the unknown by a simple tap on your device. This momentary relief of anxiety consequently draws your attention away from your partner. When Pete and Joe were in bed, Joe would attempt to speak with Pete about his day and the issues he was having with his students. Pete would respond with one-word or short answers, and Joe would become frustrated. Pete told him he was listening and did not understand Joe's frustration. I discussed the concept of active listening with Joe and Pete. Hearing and listening are different. Pete heard Joe. Pete could probably recite back Joe's complaints. *But was Pete mentally processing Joe's situation? Was Pete giving Joe's stressors enough cognitive attention to provide an appropriate response?*

ANALYSIS: PHONE AS YOUR NEW BFF

Active listening requires focusing on the person with whom you are speaking. However, have you noticed when you eat at a restaurant the number of phones placed on the table or being used? Groups of friends sit in silence as they swipe or scroll aimlessly. Couples, distracted by texts and Instagram, are completely non-present.

Perhaps you are aware that you have engaged in similar behaviors. I wonder about the point of going out in the first place. It would take less energy to sit at home, text that friend/partner, and order in some food. It would be more affordable and relaxing. An additional benefit is staying in your growfit (grey outfit) or onesie and kicking back with your legs up on the sofa. However, you made a deliberate choice. You chose to get up, get dressed, and venture outside to share in the human experience. My assumption is that you were hoping to engage in conversation with another person. However, technology, especially handheld devices and laptops, has created a change in the use of public space. People bring their laptops to coffee shops and go to restaurants to engage with others through their phone. In many ways, this seems counterintuitive. They are utilizing the public domain to concentrate on private activity. This phenomenon deserves a book of its own.

RESEARCH: HOW HUMANITY FEELS ABOUT PHONE USE

Although the perception is that people are finding it difficult to part with their phones, a survey conducted in 2015 by the Pew Research Center found 88 percent of respondents believe it's "generally" not okay to use a cell phone during dinner.[1] This study also found 82 percent of respondents say that using a phone in social settings hurts conversations. Clearly that thought process isn't hindering people from displaying and using their devices. In response to a question regarding phone use during social gatherings, 89 percent of respondents said they had done so, most often to read a text or e-mail, take a photo, or send a text. This supports the idea of classifying cell phone use as an addiction, as it represents ego-dystonic behavior. *Ego-dystonic* refers to thoughts and behaviors that are dissonant (not in agreement). Not only is the behavior impulsive, but it also conflicts with the idea that using a phone can be detrimental to interpersonal connection.

THERAPY: COMMUNICATION UTILIZING GOTTMAN

An important piece of helping Pete and Joe in therapy was to identify their shared goal. Both Pete and Joe valued quality time and support for each other.

Working from that foundation allowed for compromise, empathy, and change. Initially, we outlined the realistic facts of the relationship including the roles they each played.

Pete and Joe faced each other during this session. It was essential they learn how to communicate their needs with each other. Pete first shared with Joe what he appreciated about Joe in the relationship. Pete expressed that he felt extremely cared for by Joe. He stated, "You pick up most of the slack, ya know, do most of the chores, because I am so tired when I get home."

Pete also acknowledged that Joe was a great listener. He said, "You always know how to calm me down after a long, hard day. You genuinely care about how my day went and let me vent to you all the time!" They both smiled, sharing a private joke about those long nights of Pete expressing his frustration with his group at work.

As Pete spoke about Joe, I witnessed Joe's eyes tear up. I asked Joe what it was like to hear Pete's sentiment, and he replied that he finally felt loved in that moment. He explained, "I had no idea Pete felt this way about me or even recognized those traits that I have. It means a lot to hear that."

Next, Joe faced Pete and expressed how proud he was of the work Pete accomplishes every day. "I appreciate how hard you work to support us. Not worrying about finances is obviously incredible. Besides that, I appreciate your kindness and strength. Your drive motivates me to work harder, dream bigger, and just be better." Pete was also taken aback by Joe's words. He assumed that Joe was angered by anything related to his work, since it cost him long hours.

These words of affirmation Pete and Joe exchanged had completely disappeared from their relationship because the couple was detached from what had brought them together initially. I had them visualize their courtship, including the travel, concerts, and fancy five-course meals. They closed their eyes and imagined the beginning stage of the relationship. I asked them to feel the excitement, the passion, the longing for each other. They pictured themselves laughing at concerts and conversing for hours over five-course meals. They reflected on the giddiness of touching one another and the comfort in holding each other. That visualization exercise reminded Pete and Joe of the foundation of their relationship.

The reality of the situation was that Pete was in a demanding job he did not anticipate leaving. The wild vacations, dancing late at concerts, and spontaneous weekend trips were not realistic at that moment in their relationship. However, Pete realized over the course of this session that he too missed his deep, meaningful conversations with Joe. I assigned both partners the task of completing John Gottman's Love Maps questionnaire (see Figure 3.1).[2] Working through the questions helped Pete to realize he lacked insight into Joe's life. Their relationship had morphed into one of superficiality, primarily venting about trivial daily stressors. Joe realized he was holding onto those

THE LOVE MAPS QUESTIONS

Play this game as frequently as you'd like. The more you play, the more you'll come to understand the concept of a Love Map and the kind of information you should include about your spouse.

1. Name two of my closest friends (2)
2. What is my favorite musical group, composer, or instrument? (2)
3. What was I wearing when we first met? (2)
4. Name one of my hobbies. (3)
5. Where was I born? (1)
6. What stresses am I facing right now? (4)
7. Describe in detail what I did today, or yesterday. (4)
8. When is my birthday? (1)
9. What is the date of our anniversary? (1)
10. Who is my favorite relative? (2)
11. What is my fondest unrealized dream? (5)
12. What is my favorite website? (2)
13. What is one of my greatest fears or disaster scenarios? (3)
14. What is my favorite time of day for lovemaking? (3)
15. What makes me feel most competent? (4)
30. What is my favorite movie? (2)
31. What are some of the important events coming up in my life? How do I feel about them? (4)
32. What are some of my favorite ways to work out? (2)
33. Who was my best friend in childhood? (3)
34. What is one of my favorite magazines? (2)
35. Name one of my major rivals or "enemies." (3)
36. What would I consider my dream job? (4)
37. What do I fear the most? [4]
38. Who is my least favorite relative? (3)
39. What is my favorite holiday? (2)
40. What kinds of books do I most like to read? (3)
41. What is my favorite TV show? (2)
42. Which side of the bed do I prefer? (2)
43. What am I most sad about? (4)
44. Name one of my concerns or worries. (4)
45. What medical problems do I worry about? (2)
46. What was my most embarrassing moment? (3)

Figure 3.1 Part of John Gottman's Love Map Questionnaire. Gottman Institute. *Love Map Questionnaire.* Copyright 2016. (Used by permission of the Gottman Institute, www.gottman.com)

past memories, and although he was proud of Pete, he only showed his anger and frustration. He acknowledged he needed to work harder to be understanding, given the reality of Pete's job.

Lastly, both Pete and Joe envisioned their future. They both wanted a family. Travel was still an important aspect of their relationship, and they discussed the vacations they planned on taking with their children. Having shared goals and dreams gave them hope for the future.

THERAPY: BEHAVIORAL CHANGES

Numerous factors created stressors for the relationship aside from technology. However, technology served as a physical and emotional barrier in this relationship, by providing both Pete and Joe a convenient means to avoid addressing the lack of intimacy. Once they began addressing their fears and openly expressing their expectations of the relationship and of each other, the wall between them began to dissipate. I worked with Pete, utilizing cognitive behavioral therapy techniques, to develop and implement strategies for coping with his anxiety. As a couple, they were able to acknowledge Pete's stress and pressure to succeed at both work and in the relationship. While Pete was given space to reveal his vulnerability, Joe felt stronger in a supportive role.

We also worked with the technology. Realistically, technology would be a presence in Pete and Joe's life. After all, getting rid of technology entirely is an almost impossible task and not what either Pete or Joe wanted. Part of the intervention was to make practical small changes to help their relationship improve in big ways.

Pete identified "his favorites": those important contacts he believed needed him to respond promptly. *There were actually only two contacts from work and Joe felt empowered when Pete added him as his third.* Over dinner, Pete was then able to put his phone on "do not disturb," allowing only the primary contacts to reach him.

Pete would still come home late. However, the new rule was that both he and Joe would place their phones on airplane mode upon entering the bedroom. If Pete still had work to do, he would notify Joe and would continue to work in the living room. In essence, their bedroom became their sanctuary. The next morning, they would spend quality time together eating breakfast. Joe learned to be more flexible and to redefine the relationship. He had to accept Pete's career, which meant that quality time would be sparser and some nights he would have to fall asleep without Joe. Joe and Pete both agreed that removing their phones and computers from the bedroom enabled them to focus completely on each other and increased intimacy.

Another helpful tool was having Joe and Pete consistently discuss their dreams for the future. They started to e-mail each other places they fantasized about visiting and to text each other pictures from past vacations. These conversations allowed them to share in their common vision and reflect on positive past experiences. Technology, in this respect, was useful in promoting closeness throughout the day.

Pete and Joe were committed and motivated to work on their relationship. Their determination allowed them to follow through on these rules and to hold themselves accountable. They continued to come to therapy for several weeks for maintenance. If either Pete or Joe broke their boundary, they would openly communicate about it without being demeaning or insulting. As a therapist, I acknowledged that for Pete and Joe, removing a phone completely from the vicinity was nearly impossible. This is a prime example of how a technology-driven society directly affects relationship dynamics, and how *phone attachment is problematic.*

RESEARCH: AFTER-WORK PHONE USE

Russell Johnson, Michigan State University's assistant professor of management, and his colleagues studied participants' use of their smartphones after work hours and how that usage affected sleep time and level of energy. According to Barnes, Lanaj, and Johnson, "Smartphones are almost perfectly designed to disrupt sleep . . . because they keep us mentally engaged late into the evening, they make it hard to detach from work so we can relax and fall asleep."[3] They added how the blue light of the phone is the most disruptive of all colors of light and is known to hinder melatonin, a chemical in the body that promotes sleep. Acknowledging the impact that phone usage has on the brain is just one explanation of an individual's inability to sufficiently multitask.

Kent State University researchers Andrew Lepp, Jacob Barkley, and Jian Li, and a Kent State graduate student, Saba Salehi-Esfahani, surveyed a random sample of 454 college students to examine how different types of cell phone users experience daily leisure.[4]

They found that high-frequency cell phone users experienced significantly more leisure distress. *Leisure distress* is defined as feeling uptight, stressed, and anxious during free time. Picture yourself laying on the couch, relaxed and stress free. Perhaps you turn on the television or pick up a book. Try to imagine how much time passes before you either find your way to your phone or at least to wonder if you've received any messages. One explanation of leisure distress is that high-frequency cell phone users often feel obligated to remain constantly connected to their phones. Participants in the study described the obligation as stressful. The study suggested that the stress may be spilling over into their leisure period. Therefore, someone who holds and checks his or her phone all day can feel a sense of discomfort and agitation during his or her free time (time spent with his or her partner), making it even harder to give his or her partner his or her full attention.

CASE STUDY: LACEY'S DATING DISASTER

Lacey described a date when her date spent half the time texting on his phone. Lacey left feeling insulted and completely turned off by his behavior. She was unsure how to respond in the moment. As Lacey's therapist, I only heard her perspective and was therefore unaware of his perception of Lacey and the date in general. However, the details of the date were less important than her adverse reaction. I worked with Lacey on determining what her response meant in terms of her values on dating and preferences of behavior. Lacey's offense, anger, and overall negative response were an indication that she wanted her date's full attention. To Lacey, having her date look at his phone was a sign of disrespect. Some individuals don't mind sitting with their partner at a table scrolling social media or texting friends. Lacey, however, was significantly disturbed by his behavior. In therapy, Lacey was able to determine her personal beliefs regarding technology and dating. She felt that dating should be a technology-free environment where both parties invest their full attention in one another, showing interest and expressing empathy. This would be demonstrated through eye contact and being inquisitive, both actions that are nearly impossible to engage in when distracted by a phone.

ANALYSIS: DATING WITH A PHONE

The discomfort of going on a date and the fear of periods of silence may promote the urge to pick up a phone. The wall that technology creates is addictive and comforting. However, embracing the silence and gazing at one another is more likely to lead to an intimate connection than staring at and scrolling on your phone. It might be helpful to even acknowledge the silence and laugh about the dating process. The sole purpose of the date is for two people to get to know each other and to determine if there is potential, attraction, and flow. The use of a phone during a date can be detrimental in that mission. It distracts from the experience and prevents you from giving your date a fair chance.

RESEARCH: THE NEED TO CONNECT

Sherry Turkle, author of *Alone Together: Why We Expect More from Technology and Less from Each Other*, states:

> Across generations, technology is implicated in this assault on empathy. We've gotten used to being connected all the time, but we have found ways around

conversation—at least from conversation that is open-ended and spontaneous, in which we play with ideas and allow ourselves to be fully present and vulnerable. But it is in this type of conversation—where we learn to make eye contact, to become aware of another person's posture and tone, to comfort one another and respectfully challenge one another—that empathy and intimacy flourish. In these conversations, we learn who we are.

Of course, we can find empathic conversations today, but the trend line is clear. It's not only that we turn away from talking face to face to chat online. It's that we don't allow these conversations to happen in the first place because we keep our phones in the landscape.[5]

The first step in enhancing interpersonal relationships is becoming self-aware. For example, if people tell you that you are consistently distracted by your phone, they probably aren't lying. Do you genuinely feel that you are someone who feels the need to look at your phone when it vibrates? If so, attempt to proactively turn it off or put it on silent mode during a date or time-out with friends. If it is a habit you find difficult to resist, try to figure out why you feel such a compelling urge. Are you uncomfortable with silence? Do you feel an urgency to check social media and see the latest post? For many Millennials and Generation X'ers, not having access to a phone causes anxiety or symptoms of withdrawal. We graduated from security blankets and stuffed animals to a hand-size contraption that makes noise. Be honest with yourself if you are someone who cannot be without a phone. You can test yourself by putting your phone away for a few hours and seeing how you feel. You will recognize how attached you truly are.

Learning how to be alone without technology is the first step in transferring that behavior to interpersonal communication. According to Turkle, "We turn time alone into a problem that needs to be solved with technology."[6] A study conducted by Timothy Wilson, a psychologist at the University of Virginia, explored individuals' capacity for solitude:

> People were asked to sit in a chair and think, without a device or a book. They were told that they would have from six to 15 minutes alone and that the only rules were that they had to stay seated and not fall asleep. In one experiment, many student subjects opted to give themselves mild electric shocks rather than sit alone with their thoughts.[7]

When we are alone, we sit with our thoughts, utilizing the power of stream of consciousness. We have the ability to be creative, mindful, and present. This skillset can be easily lost, as described in the preceding case study. Without this skillset, it is extremely difficult to be present in conversation with others. Therefore, try to initially master being alone without technology. Start with a half hour and work your way up to longer lengths of time. See how this changes your sense of self and if it enhances your interpersonal relationships.

CASE STUDY: IS PHONE ADDICTION REAL?

Maya, a 23-year-old female, and Rich, a 35-year-old male, separately came to therapy because friends and family members told them they were too attached to their phones. At first, both Maya and Rich described their feelings of anger. They both refused to believe they were that attached to their devices. They lashed out at anyone who criticized them. However, after receiving interventions from multiple support networks, they decided to seek therapy. I asked each of them to describe the observations made by their family and friends.

Maya: "My friends sat me down and I was immediately nervous. I couldn't imagine what they were possibly going to tell me. They explained that I am hard to be around because of my phone attachment. They gave examples of times where I sat a table completely ignoring important updates in their lives. At first, I was hesitant and taken aback. But then I realized that I actually was unaware of those life changes they were experiencing, and if they did in fact tell me, then it was terrible that I did not hear it because I was looking at my phone."

Rich: "My immediate family sat me down and I knew exactly what they were going to say. They had all individually told me, at one point, that I was obsessed with my phone and I just ignored them. It was a different feeling, though, sitting down with all of them. It made the whole situation more serious. They told me that they couldn't take it anymore. That it was at the point where they didn't want to invite me to family functions because it was embarrassing for them how much I was on my phone. Once they started telling me the names of all the extended family members that said something, I agreed to seek some help. I never want to be an embarrassment to them and I guess I never realized how important this was to them."

ANALYSIS: THE POWER OF MINDFULNESS

The concept of phone addictions is complicated and involves a range of factors. Let's begin with the obvious: the incessant need to read text messages and answer phone calls. I have witnessed couples playing games on their phones while eating together. While observing these couples, I prayed that one person would look up and ask the other one a question, even if it was about the food. Every day a new app is created to make our lives easier in some way. Apps are useful and necessary. I checked and I have over 60 apps on my phone (some of which I have no idea what they are). With the introduction of new apps and the expansion of technology comes much more responsibility. I love that Spider-Man line: "With great power comes great responsibility." The question I pose is: Are you being digitally responsible? A group of Silicon Valley tech employees created the website DigitalResponsibility.org in order to share with young people the personal and public consequences of technology. Their defi-nition of being digitally responsible is "using technology in a way that doesn't harm others and to be aware of the impact that technology has on our health, environment, and society at large."[8]

The key to their definition is mindfulness. Mindful of what? Most impor-tantly, you need to be aware of how your use of technology is affecting yourself and others. Be aware that your behavior is signaling a message to your partner. Are you being attentive, approachable, and inquisitive? Does your body lan-guage alert your partner of your interest and concern? If you are pretending to listen while on your phone, what are you therefore implying? Ultimately, do you prioritize your phone over your relationships? For Maya and Rich, the phone obsession became problematic when it began affecting their relation-ships with friends and family. They needed to develop increased self-awareness to understand the lack of attention and support they were providing to those most important to them. A device used up their focus and energy, leaving no room for interpersonal connections.

RESEARCH: PHANTOM VIBRATION

Another factor of phone addiction is "phantom vibration." You know that feel-ing where you could have sworn you felt your phone vibrate in your pocket, even if it was on silent mode? Daniel Kruger conducted a study involving 290 U.S. college students, in which he found nearly 90 percent of them said they sometimes felt phantom phone sensations and 40 percent said it happened at least once a week.[9] According to Randi Smith, a licensed clinical social worker and associate professor of psychology at Metropolitan State University of Denver, "It's almost like a hallucination. There's a fear that we're going to miss a text, somebody is trying to reach us and we're not being responsive."[10]

From my experience, it makes sense to link this behavior to a form of separation anxiety. Individuals develop an inherent fear of being apart from their phones. They become emotionally attached. Besides the unease of not catching a call or text, there is also the feeling that something is missing. You become so reliant on the phone and simultaneously dependent on the vibra-tions that when your phone is away, on silent, or inactive, you can potentially feel a sensation.

According to the Pew Research Center, 67 percent of smartphone owners have admitted to checking their phone for calls or messages when their phone did not vibrate or ring.[11] Although cell phone addiction is not yet listed in the *Diagnostic and Statistical Manual of Mental Disorders*, fifth edition (DSM-5), research has compared it to gambling addiction, which has clearer diagnostic criteria and is included in the DSM-5.[12]

According to PsychGuides.com:

At least four of the following signs and symptoms are thought to comprise criteria for a cell phone addiction.[13] Additionally, the problematic cell phone overuse must cause significant harm in the individual's life:

1. A need to use the cell phone more and more often in order to achieve the same desired effect.
2. Persistent failed attempts to use cell phone less often.
3. Preoccupation with smartphone use.
4. Turns to cell phone when experiencing unwanted feelings such as anxiety or depression.
5. Excessive use characterized by loss of sense of time.
6. Has put a relationship or job at risk due to excessive cell phone use.
7. Tolerance.

   - Need for newest cell phone, more applications, or increased use.
   - Withdrawal, when cell phone or network is unreachable.
   - Anger.
   - Tension.
   - Depression.
   - Irritability.
   - Restlessness.

How many of these symptoms do you possess?

RESEARCH: THE CENTER FOR INTERNET AND TECHNOLOGY ADDICTION

Dr. David Greenfield is the founder of the Center for Internet and Technology Addiction (virtual-addiction.com) and an assistant clinical professor of psychiatry at the University of Connecticut School of Medicine. He is recognized as one of the world's leading voices on Internet, computer, and digital media behavior, and a pioneer concerning compulsive and addictive use. He is the author of *Virtual Addiction*, which rang an early warning bell about tech overuse when it came out in 1999.[14]

Here is a self-assessment tool he provides on his website. The website states that the Internet Abuse Test measures the impact of Internet use on your relationships and social life:[15]

1. Do you find yourself spending more time on your smartphone than you realize?
2. Do you find yourself mindlessly passing time on a regular basis by staring at your smartphone even though there might be better or more productive things to do?
3. Do you seem to lose track of time when on your cell phone?

4. Do you find yourself spending more time texting, tweeting, or e-mailing as opposed to talking to real-time people?

5. Has the amount of time you spend on your cell phone been increasing?

6. Do you secretly wish you could be a little less wired or connected to your cell phone?

7. Do you sleep with your smartphone on or under your pillow or next to your bed regularly?

8. Do you find yourself viewing and answering texts, tweets, and e-mails at all hours of the day and night, even when it means interrupting other things you are doing?

9. Do you text, e-mail, tweet, or surf the Internet while driving or doing other similar activities that require your focused attention and concentration?

10. Do you feel your use of your cell phone actually decreases your productivity at times?

11. Do you feel reluctant to be without your smartphone, even for a short time?

12. When you leave the house, do you *always* have your smartphone with you and do you feel ill-at-ease or uncomfortable when you accidentally leave your smartphone in the car or at home, or you have no service, or it is broken?

13. When you eat meals, is your cell phone always part of the table place setting?

14. When your phone rings, beeps, buzzes, do you feel an intense urge to check for texts, tweets, or e-mails, updates, and so on?

15. Do you find yourself mindlessly checking your phone many times a day even when you know there is likely nothing new or important to see?

Try taking his assessment and see how you fare. According to the website, if you answer *Yes* to more than three of the questions, then you would benefit from going on a digital diet. The website has tools and tips to better manage your Internet usage. This can be a good place to start if you want to be more self aware.

CASE STUDY: WAIT, WE HAVE TO ACTUALLY SPEAK IN PERSON?

Martin, a 24-year-old, heterosexual male, presented to therapy with generalized anxiety. He also struggled with impulsivity and anger management. Martin yearned for emotional attachment. He wanted therapy to assist him in developing skills to communicate with women. When I asked Martin about his comfort with "small talk," he asked me to provide examples to help define "small talk." I explained that it is casual conversation, such as "What's your favorite type of music?" or "What do you do for a living?" Sessions with Martin included role-playing basic conversations that would provide him with the confidence to approach a woman.

I noticed that Martin was a fan of texting, because he would receive many texts throughout the session and would immediately return to his phone when the session was over. I brought this up with him during one of our sessions.

"Martin, I notice that you enjoy texting."

He replied, "Yes, it's how my friends and I communicate." We proceeded to discuss the types of conversations he has with his friends.

He stated, "Ya know, we talk about sports, mess with each other, or they brag about sleeping with women, when it probably didn't happen [laughs]."

I wondered aloud why these types of conversations did not transfer over to in-person communication skills. After a brief pause, Martin explained that texting was easy and natural. He felt no pressure or anxiety and he was free to speak his mind. The presence of women made him nervous and the added stress of having to say the right thing in the moment was "too much for him to handle."

ANALYSIS: TECHNOLOGY AND COMMUNICATION

Technology provides an alternative medium for communicating, where you can project a different, more ideal persona. It gives you the ability to be isolated and allows you to form relationships without developing the skillset of forming face-to-face connections. In her book, *Reclaiming Conversation: The Power of Talk in a Digital Age*, Sherry Turkle discusses why the power of face-to-face communication is so important.[16] Jonathan Franzen of the *New York Times* summarized her novel.[17]

The people she interviewed have adopted new technologies in pursuit of greater control, only to feel controlled by them. The likeably-idealized selves they've created with social media leave their real selves all the more isolated. They communicate incessantly but are afraid of face-to-face conversations. They worry, often nostalgically, that they are missing out on something fundamental. Conversation carries the risk of boredom, the condition that smartphones have taught us most to fear, which is also the condition in which patience and imagination are developed.

Using technology also removes the element of nonverbal communication. Studies have shown the significance of eye contact, for example, how a lack of touch and an absence of eye contact from parents postpartum can cause symptoms of depression, anger, and alienation for their children later in life.[18] So, have we developed an inability to communicate due to technology or have distractions always been present? I had an interesting conversation with my friend's father about this topic. He brought up the similarity of men reading the newspapers at the breakfast table as a type of distraction from engaging with their spouses.

This begs the question: Is it human nature to have trouble staying focused and being easily distracted? Is it simply difficult to concentrate and has technology just heightened that propensity? The main difference, I noted, is that, in the past, humans were unable to carry around that distraction. When couples would go out to a restaurant or a Broadway show, they wouldn't carry

Photo 3.1 Distraction in the Past. Everett Collection. *Couple Reading Newspaper at Breakfast Table.* August 7, 2017. (Shutterstock.com)

Photo 3.2 Distraction Present Day. *Modern Couple.* August 7, 2017. (Pexel.com)

newspapers around with them. If someone had a newspaper in her bag, she surely wouldn't open it and read it during those activities. It was not proper etiquette or socially acceptable.

Today, we have a range of entertainment possibilities in a device small enough to fit in our pocket. We have games, articles, news, and social media all within reach. It is almost commonplace and acceptable to have your phone out at all times. There are rare moments when looking at a phone is openly judged, such as at a movie theater. The fact that it is not more widely stigmatized creates an inherent idea that it is an acceptable behavior. In other words, the thought process goes: "Everyone does it, so I'm going to feel okay staring at my phone, as well" or "I don't want to stare at people looking at their phone, so I'll just look at mine also."

RESEARCH: NONVERBAL COMMUNICATION

So how does being on your phone thwart emotional connection? Besides the obvious lack of verbal communication, nonverbal communication is also absent. Nonverbal communication is essential in illuminating the dynamics of personal relationships. Laura Guerrero and Kory Floyd define nonverbal communication in their book, *Nonverbal Communication in Close Relationships,* as "nonlinguistic messages that people exchange in interactive contexts."[19] They state that "nonverbal behaviors account for 60 to 65% of the meaning conveyed in an interpersonal exchange."[20] They explain how nonverbal communication "encompasses a broad array of visual, vocal, tactile, olfactory, gustatory, chronemic, and artifactual behaviors, many of which are routinely enacted in concert with each other to convey meaning."[21] Guerrero and Floyd point out how nonverbal (body language) and verbal communication (spoken words) often convey contradictory messages. For example, have you ever asked someone how he or she feels and he or she responds, "Great," but appear withdrawn or upset? The posture and tone can lead you to probe further despite his or her verbiage being positive.

That is one reason why face-to-face therapy is encouraged over telephone and video sessions. Therapists utilize nonverbal cues to make a complete assessment of a client's feelings and responses. Body language is a major component in all associations, not just therapeutic relationships. I have heard multiple complaints from clients lately that their physicians are spending more time dealing with their electronic health record than examining them. This is the epitome of how information gained electronically supersedes knowledge gained through personal interaction. Looking someone in the eyes, with an open stance, indicates openness and availability. If you are staring at your phone, texting, or looking at Instagram, Twitter, BuzzFeed, and others, you are indirectly expressing a lack of interest. In all aspects of life, being cognizant of the person's physical presence enhances the interpersonal relationship.

IMPLICATIONS FOR THERAPISTS

This "Implication for Therapists" section will include the initial assessment, a psychoeducation element, and a treatment approach. I chose to address the addictive nature of technology and consequential dependencies that arise. Many people are dependent on cell phones. Clients may feel uncomfortable if they leave it at home and panic if they lose it. Cell phones have become an extension of one's body, and for some, it seems a truly indispensable appendage. Investigating a person's relationship with technological devices will reveal his or her level of addiction and the optimum modality of treatment.

ASSESSMENT

When clients enter the room, they are typically not reporting technology as the presenting problem. A majority of the time, they neglect to mention technology at all in the first session (unless in relation to porn). When a couple comes in for therapy, be sure to address how technology plays a role in the relationship. The question can be brought up during a typical intake session, which might cause clients to pause and reflect. Asking them to describe and/or visualize a typical dinner or bedtime ritual could illuminate issues related to technology.

Billieux et al. discuss whether dysfunctional use of a mobile phone should be conceptualized as a "behavioral addiction."[22] They pathologize the use of a phone as dysfunctional when it leads to adverse consequences in daily life. After establishing an individual's phone use as problematic, they proceeded to discuss treatment from an addiction and psychological process model.

Their criteria for assessing phone addiction:

Criterion 1: Tolerance, meaning "a marked increase in the frequency and duration of cellular phone use to obtain satisfaction." Individuals felt the "need to substitute operative devices with the new models that appear on the market."

Criterion 2: Withdrawal. Some studies emphasized that when individuals were unable to use their mobile phone, some of them experienced emotional alterations (e.g., distress, anger, and anxiety), or intrusive or obsessive thoughts related to the mobile phone.

Criterion 3: Use more frequent or for longer than intended.

Criterion 4: Uncontrolled use. Several studies emphasized that lack of control over use (i.e., inability to stop use in response to certain situations, cues, or emotional states) is a key feature of dysfunctional mobile phone use.

Criterion 5: Wasting time because of mobile phone use.

Criterion 6: Negative impact on personal, professional, or social spheres. As emphasized previously, it has been shown that overuse of the mobile phone can have detrimental effects on various spheres of daily living (e.g., sleep disturbances, financial problems, and conflicts with family or friends).

Criterion 7: Conscious of dysfunctional use.

I found that assessing clients using this criterion is most useful when applied congruently with the psychological process-based model, which looks at the underlying factors of the addiction. For example, what are potential irrational beliefs about the self? Is low self-esteem present? What is the client's attachment style? Are they dependent or more independent? It is essential to also look at impulse control. How is the client in handling impulses in his or her day-to-day activities and behaviors?

Regardless of which assessment structure you utilize, the first step is empathizing with the phone addiction. Allowing your clients to openly discuss their dependency can be extremely helpful in developing rapport. You might be the first person to validate their symptoms.

PSYCHOEDUCATION

Once you determine there is a significant problem with phone dependency, the next step is educating your client or clients (if working with a couple). It could be helpful to cite studies that have been conducted regarding phone addictions, or educate them on how being distracted by a phone can be detrimental to relationships.

Jeffrey Hall, Nancy Baym, and Kate Miltner assessed if a partner's mobile phone use altered the level of commitment, satisfaction, and liking in the relationship. Their results indicated that "perceived adherence to participants' own internal standards—by both the participant, and the participant's relational partner—and perceived similarity between partners were more influential."[23] The implication of this study is that it is more important that individuals share with each other their personal values. What role do they feel technology should play in the relationship? For therapy purposes, the therapist can educate their clients that open communication about technology is healthy.

TREATMENT

If you decide to integrate the 12-step model, here are some tips:

1. First, enable the client to recognize and admit that he or she is experiencing an addiction problem. As a therapist, acknowledge that a person has the ability to be addicted to his or her phone (this can be in the form of touching, feeling, swiping, scrolling, and/or connecting).

2. The client surrenders to the fact that the addiction exists and decides to seek control through an outer guide (you). In this case, the client, with your help, accepts that seeking help for this type of addiction (even if it is just a general distraction) is *okay*.

3. The client practices self-observation and becomes aware of the behaviors that were part of and arose from the addiction, as well as those tools that help promote

self-restraint. Discuss in session how technology has altered daily living. Question some of your client's behaviors and how they have affected dating/relationships. Determine techniques and tools that have assisted in creating technology boundaries and/or personal limits.

4. The client will achieve self-acceptance and feel confident in his or her ability to change behaviors. Utilize therapy to track progress of acceptance, confidence, and ability to alter use of technology.

Although this might seem like a dramatic way to treat and analyze the use of technology, it would be more harmful to ignore the symptomology. Clients present with a range of issues and symptoms. Just like with any other disorder, it is your role as a therapist to empathize. If phone addiction or dependency is approached in this way, there is a more direct path for change. Additionally, this approach allows your client to feel that he or she is part of a bigger problem. By treating them for phone dependency, your clients may begin to realize this may be something their friends and peers might be struggling with, as well. This normalizes their behavior and can lead to the clients becoming more vocal and comfortable in session.

Another way to think of treatment is to compare it to a nutritionist working with a client attempting to diet. Prior to the client presenting to the nutritionist about his or her issue with weight and health, he first has to acknowledge that there is a problem. Once the problem is accepted, the nutritionist will work with the client to come up with an eating plan that is both realistic and healthy. Technology, like food, is clearly a necessity in our society. For some, it is a requirement to be available 24/7, in order to stay ahead in their career. Just like with a diet, the treatment is not to remove the phone entirely. Client will develop their boundaries for the use of technology. The change can be slow and hard. Therefore, the expectations need to be realistic and understood.

As with any presenting problem, the client needs to want the change to happen. If you work with a couple, they can discuss their agreed-upon rules of technology. Some couples determine that having a phone in the bed is a hard "no." Other couples decide that having a phone around during mealtimes is unacceptable. Regardless, the couple needs to reach a compromise as a team and the therapist can facilitate that discussion.

SUMMARY

In conclusion, different phases of life and professions bring varied responsibilities, many of which increasingly require consistent connection to devices. Technology is quickly expanding into fields that previously did not demand interaction. For example, medical professionals now use electronic health records, which requires having technology accessible in the exam room.

Competitive job markets drive a need to maintain the perception of availability. Therapists need to be conscious of the reality of young professionals to help them distinguish between what is being demanded from their employers versus themselves.

Balancing professional and personal life is becoming more difficult as employers have the capacity to reach staff in the bedroom and the bathroom. It is worth the struggle to avoid developing bad habits from the onset of a relationship by discerning the antecedents of conflicts related to the use of technology. Structuring time but enabling flexibility is crucial. Giving couples language to identify and communicate boundaries regarding the use of technology will be helpful in facilitating professional and personal growth. Partners should not be at odds with the other. Each individual's area of growth has the potential to positively influence the other when open and honest communication is present.

Chapter 4

TECHNO-JEALOUSY, AFFAIRS, AND PORN

CASE STUDY: SOPHIE AND JACKSON

Sophie, a 35-year-old heterosexual female, and Jackson, a 34-year-old heterosexual male, presented for therapy. Sophie's goal for therapy was to increase their emotional connection, while Jackson wanted more physical intimacy. They had been married for nine years and had two sons, ages 4 and 1. They met on JDate, a site for Jewish Singles to connect. Sophie was 28 years old and was getting her master's in education. Jackson was 29 years old and was working in advertising. At that point in Sophie's life, she felt pressured to find a partner because all of her friends were either in relationships or married. She felt that Jackson was a good fit, as his passivity balanced out her wild nature and they shared similar goals and values.

During their first year of courtship, they texted each other every day and didn't go to sleep without a goodnight phone call. Sophie and Jackson got engaged a year after meeting and moved in with one another. According to Jackson, the relationship noticeably changed once they moved in together. They started "missing each other less" and having less intercourse.

A few years into their marriage, Jackson had an emotional affair with a woman in his office. The affair involved texting throughout the day and messaging each other via Facebook at night. Jackson stated that the affair was a result of feeling constantly ignored by Sophie. He also described that he felt a lack of positive affirmation from Sophie. He longed for her to say, "I love you," "You're amazing," or "I'm proud of you."

Sophie felt unappreciated and unloved. She felt that she would not be able to open up to Jackson physically without an emotional connection. She felt that Jackson was not "present," meaning he did not actively listen to her concerns, feelings, and opinions. She felt that he was always distracted.

Despite Jackson terminating the affair, Sophie was unable to view Jackson as an "intimate partner." She felt anxious when she saw him on his phone and she got urges to check his Facebook page and to snoop his text messages. She felt that she needed to regain trust in Jackson and confidence in the relationship in order to move past the affair.

ANALYSIS: WHAT HAPPENED TO THE RELATIONSHIP?

Jackson and Sophie utilized texting as a means to show affection and interest during the first year of dating. However, as soon as they moved in together they stopped making an effort to communicate with each other. They both assumed that living together meant that spending quality time and having meaningful conversations would happen naturally. However, their busy schedules, paired with the lack of their familiar texting banter, led to a downward spiral in the relationship. Jackson met his coworker, and they began texting after work hours. Jackson's need to feel heard and admired was achieved with his coworker's texts. He was admittedly looking for an emotional attachment, something he felt was missing in his marriage.

Like Jackson, many of my clients who seek out affairs, whether physical or emotional, wish to fill an empty void. Their relationship demise occurs because both partners stop paying attention to each other and are unprepared to reconstruct the relationship dynamics after the move.

ANALYSIS: SOPHIE'S TECH-JEALOUSY

Jackson's use of his phone and Facebook were intensifying Sophie's jealousy. The affair revealed issues in the relationship; however, the physical presence of technology and the tension that it created is what drove them to therapy. His use of technology provoked feelings of mistrust and anger, and created a volatile relationship.

Sophie and Jackson presented as a committed couple, but they had conflicting needs that were not being met. Exploring Sophie's jealousy in the presence of technology was the first goal. These devices were instruments that enabled her lover and partner to share his day with other women. Therapy helped Sophie get past the obsessive checking behavior and overcome the threatening feelings that emerged when Jackson checked his phone and computer. Sophie was given a range of tools to help her develop trust and to associate the devices with positive thoughts and meanings.

ANALYSIS: TECHNOLOGY AND JACKSON'S EMOTIONAL AFFAIR

For Jackson, technology in itself did not instigate the emotional affair; however, it did provide the ability to continue the affair in secrecy. Texting allowed Jackson to easily connect with his coworker after work hours. What started as a harmless work relationship developed into a deeper connection over texting. The lack of attention he was receiving at home from Sophie was replaced by the validation and words of affection he obtained through texts.

Once Sophie became aware of the affair and realized that he maintained his hidden relationship through messaging, her insecurity and jealousy developed. Since her discovery, she associated him being on his phone with deceit and cheating. Jackson felt frustrated because he had to relentlessly justify being on his phone. Despite ending the affair, he felt there was nothing he could do to prove himself to Sophie. He was forced to show Sophie his text activity and computer history. Additionally, her snooping made him feel violated. This was not a sustainable pattern and would inevitably cause resentment. Jackson needed to feel trusted. Even more than that, he desired words of affirmation from Sophie in order to feel loved, valued, and heard.

ANALYSIS: CAN JEALOUSY BE GOOD FOR YOUR RELATIONSHIP?

In Sophie and Jackson's case, technology created an uncomfortable dynamic where they physically could not be in the same room together with a cell phone or computer. Sophie's jealousy of technology's presence was unhealthy, as it prevented her from focusing at home. She found herself obsessing about Jackson and his phone especially when he was physically present. This feeling was not sustainable, as technology would never be completely absent from their lives. As Sophie became more spiteful about Jackson's use of technology, he withdrew further to avoid conflict. He felt he had to be secretive when utilizing his phone or computer to avoid making Sophie upset, but this further promoted secrecy and deception.

Although, jealousy was harmful in their relationship, in a way it was also helpful since it triggered their decision to seek therapy. It made an emotional relationship issue become more concrete and definable. Technology was a presence that could not be ignored. Sophie's discomfort around Jackson's phone and computer caused a tense vibe in the house and the awkwardness lingered in the air. When jealousy began to control their lives, they decided outside help was needed.

There is a fine line between helpful jealousy and hurtful jealousy. Helen Fisher, a biological anthropologist states, "A little bit of jealousy in a healthy relationship is fine." It is understandable to value your partner and feel uncomfortable with the thought of him or her connecting to another individual.

Fisher, author of *Why We Love*, affirms: "It's going to wake you up. When you're reminded that your mate is attractive and that you're lucky, it can stimulate you to be nicer [and] friendlier."[1]

Therefore, jealousy can even fuel passion in a relationship. The question is: Does technology add too much fuel to the fire?

Jealousy comes in many forms. It can stem from your partner's successful career and/or how much money they make, or because your partner is more attractive than you, or perhaps they are healthier than you are, or they work out more. Jealousy might be pronounced when your partner gets attention or gives attention to another person.

Technology creates supplemental channels for communication. In addition to worrying about whom our partner is communicating with in person, there is the fear of who he or she is texting, "tindering (swiping on the dating app called Tinder)," poking, messaging, sending pictures to, and so on. More outlets = more anxiety.

However, Sophie did not express jealousy regarding Jackson's actions or behavior. The jealousy was directed toward the presence of the devices. In other words, her techno-jealousy instilled anger, frustration, and insecurity. The instruments themselves had enough negative connotations that simply seeing them in a room with Jackson caused her fear and anxiety.

So when does jealousy become debilitating to the relationship?

1. When it is chronic,
2. When it is harmful,
3. When it produces anxiety, and
4. When it creates insecurity.

THERAPY: ALTERING THE CONVERSATION

Tech isn't going anywhere. New apps are being created daily, and the ability to connect through devices is getting easier. Working with Sophie on her jealousy initially required her acceptance that technology would remain a presence in their lives. Phones and computers are fundamental components in communication and in achieving professional success.

Sophie was not necessarily seeking a solution for her jealousy from Jackson, as he assumed. She wanted to feel validated that her concerns were understandable. When Sophie appeared skeptical about his texting, Jackson would immediately become defensive. Sophie never expressed her insecurity outright, but became quiet and passive aggressive and withdrawn. Jackson would thrust his phone in her face to provide proof of innocence. He believed that the more times he "proved innocence," the more trustworthy he would become. We role-played how the situation could play out differently.

Jackson noticed Sophie's distress and discomfort. She became passive aggressive. Jackson responded, "What . . . are you upset because I'm texting?"

We practiced a different approach. I asked Sophie, "What would it look like, in this moment, to compromise?"

"I don't know what that means," she said.

"I wonder," I prompted, "If you could tell Jackson what you're feeling when you see him texting."

Sophie:	"So . . . I'm feeling a little nervous with you on your phone."
Jackson:	"I know, I'm sorry. I wish there was something I could do or say."
Sophie:	"I know, and I'm sorry to keep questioning you. I know it's annoying. I just am scared."
Jackson:	"I know and I get that. It makes sense that you feel that way and I feel terrible that I caused it."
Sophie:	"Thanks for saying that. I know that it will go away with time."
Jackson:	"Me, too. Just know that I love you and will never do anything. I won't risk losing you again."
Sophie:	"Thank you, that means a lot."

This type of conversation will most likely not happen every time Jackson is on his phone. However, when Jackson provided validation by saying "It makes sense," and when he empathized by saying "I feel terrible," it led to a calmer, more loving interaction. This type of dialogue gives them the opportunity to express feelings instead of hiding behind defenses. They also realized during the session that nonverbal cues, such as facing each other in an open stance, helped show their genuineness.

THERAPY: PUTTING A POSITIVE SPIN ON TECH

Sophie confessed that she had unintentionally disregarded Jackson after the kids were born. She became preoccupied with providing them with emotional and physical attention and forgot that her partner also needed that support.

She recognized that she needed to validate him with words of affirmation, in order for him to feel valued. In an attempt to use technology in a positive way, I had Sophie and Jackson text each other throughout the day with loving, caring, supportive, and endearing messages. These texts not only demonstrated their commitment and support for one another but also brought back memories of the honeymoon stage of their relationship. I advised Sophie to text Jackson every time she felt nervous or insecure. Instead of asking him where he was and what he was doing, I told her to text him a few words of affirmation, such as "You're incredible," "I love how you brought me coffee today," or

"Thank you for working so hard, it's inspirational." We were able to work up a list that Sophie thought Jackson would appreciate, and she kept that list handy to check every time she was at a loss.

As a response to her words of affirmation, Jackson texted her back with words of encouragement, support, and love. He texted her messages like "I'm thinking about you," "You're an amazing wife," or "I'm excited to see you later."

This technique served three purposes. Jackson felt more secure that Sophie valued him as a partner and was appreciative of his hard work. It gave him more confidence in the relationship and that it was going in the right direction.

Simultaneously, Sophie developed new associations for technology, which helped rebuild her trust. Sophie began to redefine technology as a tool for them to communicate the appreciation they felt for each other. It reduced her fear that Jackson was looking elsewhere, which increased her trust in him and the relationship.

Lastly, their texting banter brought them back to the exciting, flirty, initial stages of the relationship. It reminded them that they still had chemistry that had been lost over time.

RESEARCH: WHY ENGAGE IN AN INTERNET RELATIONSHIP?

Technology can make it easy to cheat. It provides people easy access and multiple opportunities to engage in infidelity. Individuals can connect on an emotional level and sext in secrecy. Without the face-to-face physical aspect, an online intimate relationship may remove feelings of guilt. However, despite the absence of physical contact, cyber relationships fulfill many needs without having to leave one's physical space.

Apps that provide video and messaging can help build and maintain long-distance relationships. They provide a myriad of opportunities for cross-cultural interactions. Partners who need to travel are able to stay in touch with each other. Physical distance is no longer the barrier it once was. Greater accessibility sometimes requires increased discipline and restraint.

The Internet provides us with the triple A engine. Internet-based technology is unique due to its easy *access, affordability*, and the *anonymous* platform it provides.[2] Individuals who engage in Internet affairs are constantly surrounded by technology, which makes communicating with their side partner easy to hide. There is also no cost, especially if the relationship remains online, which makes it more enticing. Their partners will not catch them withdrawing funds or utilizing the credit card in conspicuous locations. Individuals who describe these experiences explain that their biggest concern concerns phone bills. The anonymity is also important to many people seeking online affairs. Many apps allow you to create profiles with fake usernames and information. You can maintain confidentiality and have a separate life without anyone knowing.

Technology brings a whole new meaning to cheating. It provides intimate access to people regardless of physical proximity. People could be drawn into a relationship without effort or purposefully seek out a relationship without feeling as if it is betraying their partner.

ANALYSIS: APPS AND AFFAIRS

Apps such as Ashley Madison, Tiger-Text, and Vaulty Stocks make cheating easier. These apps allow individuals to find partners in their areas. Profiles include location, age, and relationship status (see example in Figure 4.1 from Ashley Madison). Members can continue their relationships online or decide to meet in person.

Although Jackson was not specifically using these apps, his affair was still enabled by technology. A study conducted in 2014 looked at how the use of technology can make infidelity more efficient. The researchers found:

> Secrets from partners and the ability to keep certain information private was a key issue in sexting behavior because "people can hide sexts, messages, contacts, etc." Second, trust was also noted as an issue in part because of the access that it provides to others and distractions. Related to secrets from one's partner, infidelity and jealousy were noted widely by the participants as issues created by sexting. Participants also wrote about the ease of infidelity through sexting because sexting makes it easy to cheat, temptation of sexting another woman or man and being able to put your phone on privacy and that it provides another outlet for infidelity. Part of the reason is that there is "little chance of being caught or monitored" when infidelity occurs through mobile phones.[3]

In other words, technology creates a platform of privacy—a haven for those looking outside their marriage.

Although an Internet relationship may seem inauthentic, flirting and intimacy can certainly occur and develop. Specific behaviors may include sharing private details of one's life and/or relationship with someone, and engaging in cybersex or flirting.[4] In Jackson's case, he utilized texting with his coworker to develop an emotional closeness by expressing his feelings, needs, and dreams.

RESEARCH: CYBER INFIDELITY

Dr. Marlene Wasserman is a clinical sexologist, couples and sex therapist, and author of *Cyber Infidelity: The New Seduction*. She utilized the database of Ashley Madison to conduct research on cyber infidelity.[5] So, what exactly is cyber infidelity? According to Dr. Wasserman, it is a process engaged in by two or maybe more people who are in an already-committed relationship. They use synchronous and asynchronous computer-mediated material, such as e-mails,

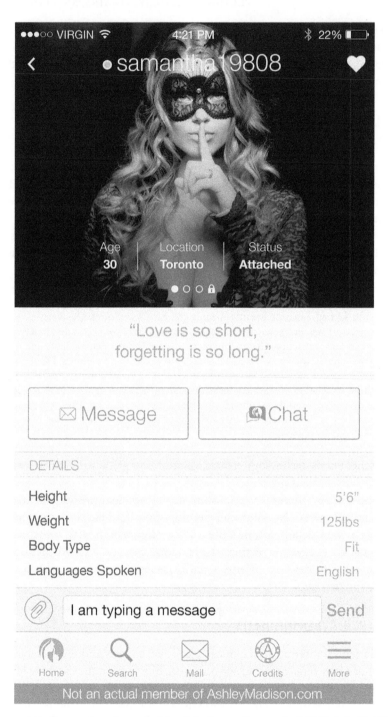

Figure 4.1 Screenshot from Ashley Madison. *Samantha19808*. July 7, 2017.
(Used by permission of Ashley Madison Media)

texts, or even Skype, to be able to communicate with each other. It's always done in a secretive manner and violates the very principles that we know to be a part of traditional relationships: monogamy, fidelity, and commitment. She adds that it is clearly another form of how people relate to one another that needs to be studied and better understood.[6]

In order to adequately assess and understand cyber infidelity, Dr. Wasserman created a profile of a married man and a single woman. She went live for two years and administered five different surveys through the app. A total of 62,600 individuals responded to the survey, including 21,039 women. They were between the ages of 18 and 55, mostly married, heterosexual, and from five different countries. The questions she posed were:

- What is cyber infidelity?
- Is it just recreational fun?
- Does it break our traditional vows of marriage?
- Should we be flexible and integrate it into our lives?
- What is it that we are expecting from our relationships?

During Dr. Wasserman's two years on the app she felt guiltless, even though she was engaging with married men. She felt happy and her self-esteem increased. She stated that it never affected her daily life. Part of the appeal was the variety of platforms on which she could access a cyber lover or chat, at a moment's notice. It was also affordable in that she didn't have to pay for clothes or meals, and it was fun. She enjoyed the anonymity and the new form of communication, which she named "hyperpersonal-intimacy." This describes the trend of online relationships in which they begin as an innocuous chat and then shift to sharing very deep intimacies. She stated that she felt more intimate with her cyber lovers than with the person lying next to her.

Dr. Wasserman also discussed how the Internet is helpful for those who are conflict-avoidant. The relationships she formed were sexy and playful. Internet relationships provided her with independence and freedom as opposed to the feeling of being domesticated "with a person you know almost too well."[7]

According to her survey, married men signed onto the website for no-strings-attached sex, adventure, and sexual variety, and were not looking for emotional connection. Women felt sexually bored, were also seeking no-strings-attached sex, and were also not seeking an emotional connection. What was interesting about the research was that the women stated they were looking for satisfactory sex, which they defined as kissing and cuddling. Dr. Wasserman found different consequences for men and women who formed relationships online. Women, while enjoying satisfactory sex, tended to fall in love with their cyber partner. Men felt more inhibited online and therefore shared more personal information with their online lover than with their partner. This increased attachment to the online partner and distanced them from their relationship.

In an interview with me, Dr. Wasserman discussed the pain that online affairs cause for relationships. Feelings of betrayal, exclusion, shame, and humiliation were elucidated in her research. Post-affair, partners experience a decrease in safety and security, and an increase in vulnerability. She explained that unlike face-to-face affairs, Internet affairs provide visual evidence in forms of words, pictures, and videos that can be extremely hurtful to see.

In terms of treatment, Dr. Wasserman suggests exploring the self-identified motivation for going online to seek a relationship. She also finds that it is important for partners to define cyber infidelity, since some individuals genuinely feel that what they are engaging in is not a form of cheating. These conversations might promote a discussion of sexual fantasies, as individuals might be looking to expand their sexual repertoire and feel that their partner would be disinterested. Partners might also begin a discussion on monogamy, openness, and boundaries. The secrecy could be the main cause of concern and not the need to engage in outside relationships.

JEALOUSY AND PORN

Case Study: Terry Crews

In 2016, Terry Crews, actor and former American football player, revealed in a series of Facebook videos that he was addicted to pornography and had to go to rehab for the problem. He stated that his addiction started at age 12 and almost cost him his wife. "If day turns into night and you are still watching, you probably got a problem," Crews explained of his addiction. He felt that porn gave him a sense of entitlement that the "world owed him something, and his wife owed him sex."

ANALYSIS: ACCORDING TO AASECT

Porn has become an increasingly popular topic of discussion in the news and mainstream media. Arguments about whether one can be addicted to porn or whether it is a diagnosable condition have surfaced in the mental health community. According to a recent mission statement from the American Association of Sexuality Educators, Counselors and Therapists (AASECT):

> AASECT: 1) does not find sufficient empirical evidence to support the classification of sex addiction or porn addiction as a mental health disorder, and 2) does not find the sexual addiction training and treatment methods and educational pedagogies

to be adequately informed by accurate human sexuality knowledge. Therefore, it is the position of AASECT that linking problems related to sexual urges, thoughts or behaviors to a porn/sexual addiction process cannot be advanced by AASECT as a standard of practice for sexuality education delivery, counseling or therapy.[8]

ANALYSIS: EASE OF ACCESS

One clear impact of technology on porn is the ease of access. Regardless of whether you are at work, at home, or on an airplane, you can access porn using today's technology. No more sneaking *Playboy* magazines from your mom or dad's dresser. Porn can be found in the blink of an eye on the Internet. If you put "free porn" into Google, you have a wide range of options in seconds. Being able to find and watch porn with zero effort can be problematic for certain individuals. Especially for those who suffer from impulsivity, a lack of boundaries, and/or an addictive personality, it can lead to difficulty focusing during the day. I agree with AASECT that it is not always helpful to pathologize consensual sexual problems for treatment purposes. However, some people, who cannot restrain from acting upon these urges, may benefit from therapies developed to treat addictive behaviors. These include AA 12-Step programs and cognitive behavioral therapy. For those who tend to have difficulty controlling impulses, having the technology with them 24/7 becomes a true challenge.

ANALYSIS: PORN'S EFFECT ON RELATIONSHIPS

Porn as education: Watching porn can be an inaccurate way for a person to become educated about sex. Many clients present to therapy venting about their sex lives. Their partner doesn't last long enough or make the right noises, and sometimes certain positions are uncomfortable. After conducting a sexual history, I determined that a majority of clients learn about sex from porn. After my clients discover that sex is not exactly "porn sex," they become disappointed and confused.

> You mean that it doesn't just slip right in and a woman doesn't always make those loud noises?—Brian, 26

The porn industry is changing, and filmmakers are attempting to make porn more realistic. However, in the meantime, if your sex education is only from porn, you might be extremely disappointed and place blame on yourself or your partner.

"I'm jealous of porn": Feelings of jealousy might emerge as a result of your partner watching porn. Clients express feeling inadequate, insecure, and uncomfortable that their partner is finding pleasure watching another person naked or engaging in various sexual acts. Sentiments such as *Am I not good enough?* or *Does he not find me attractive?* are typically voiced during a session.

RESEARCH: PORN TOGETHER OR APART?

Amanda Maddox, Galena Rhoades, and Howard Markman conducted a study in which they investigated the associations between viewing sexually explicit material (SEM) and relationship functioning.[9] Their participants were a random sample of 1,291 unmarried individuals in romantic relationships.

Couples in which neither partner viewed pornography reported higher relationship quality than did those in which one or both partners viewed pornography alone. Couples in which partners consumed pornography only together, however, reported similar relationship quality to those who never viewed pornography. They also reported higher dedication to the relationship and more sexual satisfaction compared to solitary consumers.

So watching pornography as a couple can be a tool to increase sexual chemistry and intimacy. Discussing feelings that emerge while watching porn can increase arousal. Some couples state in session that hearing their partner describe the type of body or scenario he or she finds attractive can be arousing. So, instead of *Game of Thrones*, try some Pornhub before bed.

RESEARCH: HONESTY AND PORN

A team of Canadian researchers, Marley Resch and Kevin Alderson, investigated honesty regarding pornography use and mutual consumption between partners.[10] They found that female partners who believed their male partners to be honest about their pornography use reported higher relationship satisfaction and less distress than female partners who experienced dishonesty from their male partners.

If partners practice honesty in relation to using pornography, it could be associated with greater reports of relationship satisfaction, thus increasing happiness, pleasure, and bonding of romantic couples. This makes sense, as the behavior isn't hidden, shady, or private. When it is kept completely secret, it can lead to shame and increased jealousy. I've heard this sentiment from multiple clients:

> If it's not about me, then why is he keeping it so hidden? or Why does he act like he is on an FBI mission when he watches porn? It makes me feel like he is doing something wrong or cheating in some way.

I'm not suggesting you call your partner and say "Oh, hey, by the way, I'm about to watch some porn."

TALKING ABOUT PORN USE

Communication in relationships regarding pornography is absent, and pornography has become a "hush hush" act. Instead of an open, enlightening, and perhaps arousing discussion regarding fantasy and pleasure, partners keep their pornography an individual and hidden pleasure. If there is anything these studies prove, it is that there is no right answer. Some couples might benefit from enjoying pornography together, while other couples might discuss and agree upon on a no-porn rule. Regardless of the decision, communicating about pornography is a positive way to increase relationship closeness.

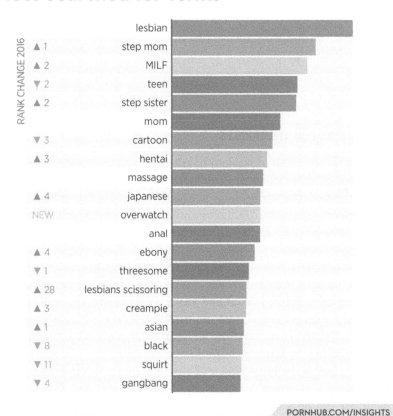

Figure 4.2 Pornhub's 2016 Year in Review. *Most Searched for Terms.* January 4, 2017. (Used by permission of Pornhub Insights)

It can be helpful to disclose to your partner what type of porn you watch as a Segway to discuss fantasy and desire. People are interested in a range of porn, which was recently published in Pornhub's Year in Review (Figure 4.2). Some couples may choose to reenact or role-play the fantasy.

If you are interested in additional material on the use of porn, Marty Klein, licensed marriage and family therapist and certified sex therapist, recently published a book on porn, titled *His Porn, Her Pain*.[11]

RESEARCH: PORNHUB YEAR IN REVIEW—WHAT'S "IN" RIGHT NOW?[12]

Total visits to Pornhub: 23 billion

Per day: 64 million

Per hour: 2.6 million

Per minute: 44,000

Per second: 729

For the second year in a row, "lesbian" was the number-one search term worldwide.

"Step mom" was second (up one spot from last year), followed by "MILF," up two places from 2015.

"Lesbian scissoring" jumped a couple dozen positions to make the top 20 this year.

Jamaica had the highest proportion of female visitors in the world at 46 percent.

IMPLICATIONS FOR THERAPISTS

Therapists will find that technology has the potential of becoming the influential and powerful bedfellow in a relationship. Jealousy, competition, and anger can emerge due to a partner's involvement with his or her phones, laptops, tablets, and/or computers. Technology often becomes a compelling distraction from a relationship. Unlike human partners, technology is continually accessible and predictable.

Therapists ascertain the basis of the jealous feelings by navigating the historical perspective from both sides. The sexual assessment needs to include how each person learned about and views pornography. This will illuminate whether the partners define porn differently, and may help answer the question of whether the porn-watching itself is the problem or if there is a fear that porn is replacing the intimate relationship.

Jealousy due to the involvement of a partner's porn use is even more convoluted because it provides fulfillment of an intimate need. One's desire to masturbate can be a result of a range of feelings. Relief from stress, understanding of one's body, sexual gratification, and fantasizing are just a few of the motivations behind self-pleasure. The act of watching porn is not necessarily a result of the lack of sexual interest in a partner or attraction for that partner.

Often therapists feel that the partner using porn is the only one who requires treatment and may tend not to fully explore the responses of the other partner. Jealousy is a complex feeling that is often deeply rooted. It may eclipse other feelings, including those of self-loathing and insecurity. It is usually depicted as the fear of loss of the relationship or a partner due to his or her involvement with or attraction to another person. However, it can also be triggered by a partner's sexual satisfaction through pornography. Scrutinizing the roots of the jealousy with a couple is a labor-intensive process, but often leads to greater understanding and forgiveness. Sometimes the act of masturbation itself is held in disdain because of cultural and/or religious beliefs. Pornography may also be deemed immoral due to these convictions. These need to be explored and shared by the couple. However, regardless of the reason for masturbation and pornography use, a partner needs to feel valued and in some way irreplaceable.

QUESTIONS FOR CONSIDERATION

1. Understand the history of the jealousy. Was there an incident that directly triggered feelings of jealousy (e.g., Jackson's emotional affair)? Relationship history is also important. Inquire if there was jealousy or infidelity in previous relationships.

2. What is the fear behind the jealousy? What will happen? (For example, if a partner is watching porn, what does that mean about your relationship?)

3. How does technology play a role in the jealousy? Is this acknowledged by the individual and/or the couple?

4. Do you feel that porn replaces you as a sexual partner?

TECHNIQUES TO CONSIDER: ADDRESSING JEALOUSY

Clients will begin to explore with each other the root and object of the jealousy. A conversation with a partner would begin with "I" sentences and describe their emotions. Some phrases might be "I am feeling hurt and not heard" or "I feel lonely because our time together is short and is consumed by the use of technology" or "I feel insecure when you watch porn. I worry that you are not interested in or attracted to me."

This can set the path for actions such as "Can we watch porn together?" or "Can we be honest with each other when we want to self-pleasure?" Partners might ask each other why they feel the need to masturbate and watch porn. This also gives them space to negate negative thoughts and to affirm feelings for one another.

Jealousy regarding technology is most likely a result of an underlying fear or concern. Therefore, when partners share and discuss the impact of technology on their relationship, it may become a catalyst for uncovering underlying issues. Active listening, explained in a previous chapter, can be the most effective way to produce change. Once the meaning beneath the jealousy is explored, the couple, with the help of the therapist, will implement solutions to reduce anxiety and promote closeness.

Conversations regarding jealousy can be especially difficult. There is a high level of vulnerability in admitting that type of emotion. Individuals may fear their partner's responses, especially if they do not receive reassurance. Therapists have to step in when appropriate and acknowledge the difficulty of the topic. This can help create a safe space for both individuals to be honest with one another.

TECHNIQUES TO CONSIDER: SCHEDULING TECH-FREE DATE NIGHT

Scheduling is a helpful tool for couples, in general, especially when technology plays a detrimental role in the relationship. For example, some couples schedule date nights once a week, during which all forms of technology are turned off and put away. However, it is essential for clients to be realistic. Some occupations require individuals to be connected at certain times at night. Additionally, studying for tests or writing papers might entail students working well into the evening. Ultimately, this technique is adapted to fit the lives of the couple. It is detrimental to the relationship to create rules and boundaries and to plan date nights that are impossible to implement. That creates more frustration and disappointment. A therapy session is helpful for the couple to figure out a balance that works for both partners.

For example, Sophie and Jackson loved to cook and would schedule a night when they would pick out a recipe and work together in the kitchen. When technology was removed from the equation, Sophie felt more connected to Jackson. She recognized that his attention was on her and her anxiety dissipated. Sophie and Jackson found mutual pleasure in cooking and spending quality time together. Sophie found herself admiring Jackson in the kitchen and would touch him lightly in passing. Although she did not feel ready to have intercourse with him, Jackson appreciated her openness and physical expression. Regardless of how busy Jackson and Sophie were, they acknowledged that they both needed to eat and were passionate about finding new types of food to indulge in. Cooking as a couple is a fun, interactive, and potentially sensual experience. Certain foods are aphrodisiacs. So if you're working with a couple like Sophie and Jackson, try encouraging them to find recipes that include aphrodisiacal spices to enhance the evening.

TECHNIQUES TO CONSIDER: NORMALIZING PORN

Helping individuals and couples feel less shame about watching or using porn will be beneficial for clients who are either uneducated or insecure. Below are steps to assist clients during the session:

1. Begin by asking the couple their ideas and thoughts regarding porn.

2. Have the couple converse with each other, so that they can mirror the dialogue at home.

3. They can discuss their hesitations and fears, while also addressing their fantasies, in a safe but direct way.

4. Lastly, they can create rules to implement in the home. For example, some couples decide that pornography can be viewed only when their partner is out of the home. Other couples only want to watch together. Having this type of conversation, in which the couple co-creates rules and boundaries, can make each partner feel heard, respected, and secure.

TECHNIQUES TO CONSIDER: PSYCHOSEXUAL EDUCATION

The stigmatization of porn in various cultures can lead to feelings of shame and guilt, creating a need for secrecy. This can later be transferred to a relationship with a partner, in which the person feels that he or she has to keep the act completely separate from the "bedroom." Education can be helpful in reducing those feelings of shame and explaining how porn can be utilized to promote closeness and a shared experience.

Jealousy is a normal response when someone feels inadequate or less than the woman or man on the screen. It also occurs when the type of sexual behavior viewed on screen is so vastly different from what the couple is experiencing. This can lead to feelings of guilt by the person viewing the porn and feelings of jealousy and inadequacy by the partner. Addressing this phenomenon and normalizing it for the couple can help lead into deeper discussions of boundaries, fantasies, and desires in the relationship.

SUMMARY

Jealousy is a complicated emotion, and the degree to which it is experienced can vary greatly between individuals. Infidelity and addictions have always been major obstacles to maintaining intimate relationships. However, now that some affairs begin online, the constant presence of technology can also be a trigger, reminding the partner of the indiscretion. Couples have to assert boundaries and regain trust that their partner is not straying simply when utilizing their devices. Having easy access means increased opportunities to meet and connect with partners. Therefore, people who have a propensity to act on their impulse are especially at risk for engaging in infidelity. Exploring the self- identified motivation for going online to seek a relationship is the first step in treatment.

Porn is a topic that is often debated among partners, especially when it instills jealousy. Porn can be a fun outlet for some, yet an obsession for others. Some couples enjoy watching porn together, while others identify it with feelings of guilt and shame. Certain fantasies might produce feelings of embarrassment and insecurity. Jealousy shows its face when a partner feels neglected or undesired. Open communication regarding porn use will enable partners to be empathetic and open-minded to each other's fears and desires.

Partners vary in their level of phone dependency. Phones fulfill particular needs at different stages of life. Individuals who are in transitional stages, like moving from dating to commitment may be more likely to continue to relate to their phone as their lifeline when in fact, they already have the physical presence of a partner. Identifying these factors and encouraging the expression of vulnerabilities could enrich the relationship and promote emotional growth.

Chapter 5

SOCIAL MEDIA, EXPECTATIONS, AND REALITY

CASE STUDY: THE PRESSURE ON JUDY AND PAUL

Judy, a 29-year-old heterosexual female, and Paul, a 29-year-old heterosexual male, presented to therapy with uncertainty about their future. Having met in a bar, they enjoyed two years of passionate, stimulating dates. After those two years, Paul nervously broached the topic of moving in together, and Judy responded with excitement and positivity. Simultaneously, they adopted a golden retriever, sharing the responsibility of caring for it. Both Paul and Judy felt optimistic about the future.

I asked what brought them in for therapy. Judy described feeling "stuck" and frustrated that the relationship was not progressing. She stated, "Everyone around me is getting engaged. I don't feel ready necessarily but feel like I need to be in that stage of life. It makes me question where we are at in our relationship."

I then turned to Paul who responded, "I get where Judy is coming from but I just want to get engaged when it feels right. Things are great now and I don't feel a need to rush."

After their joint session, I met with them each individually. I spoke with Judy about the pressure she was feeling and where it came from. She explained, "I feel the most insecure from social media. When I see photos of people getting engaged, pregnant, or moving into houses, I get a pit in my stomach. I'm scared that those things will never happen for me." I asked if she felt prepared to get engaged emotionally. She thought for a few seconds and said, "Not really. I am looking to change careers and am dealing with family stuff. I can't explain really what I feel, it's just hard seeing all these other couples moving forward."

Paul, in his individual session, stated, "I'm very happy in my relationship with Judy. I think we're great together. It's just that I started law school last year and I want to feel more stable in my career. I want to focus on the present and not the future. I'm just not sure I am on the same page as Judy."

ANALYSIS: JUDY AND PAUL'S RELATIONSHIP

Judy and Paul have a very solid foundation. They openly communicate their fears, concerns, and expectations. In their day-to-day routine, both Judy and Paul appear to feel confident in their relationship and with each other. In therapy, they demonstrated their love and affection by holding hands and voicing words of affirmation. They shared essential values, such as the importance of family and their love for travel and independence.

Their commitment to one another was clear in their decision to seek therapy. Both Judy and Paul were emphatic that they would put in the effort to make the relationship work. It was important to each of them that they fulfilled the needs of their partner. They sought strategies to stay in the present and tools to communicate more effectively about their future.

ANALYSIS: SOCIAL MEDIA PRESSURE

Judy and Paul were motivated to accomplish their personal and professional goals prior to embarking on engagement.

Judy could not ignore the constant posts on Facebook, Instagram, and Snapchat of other couples (even ones she did not know) appearing to be in further stages in their relationships. They were making her overanalyze the status of her relationship and question her future with Paul. To Judy, not being engaged was an indication that her relationship was stagnating and that she was falling behind others. Since she tended to be competitive, she responded viscerally to these posts and could not seem to control feeling inadequate. This became her insurmountable reality despite being in a loving, supportive relationship.

Paul, on the other hand, was desperately trying to balance the demands of law school with fulfilling the role of a supportive boyfriend. No time for Facebook or social media, Paul was struggling to maximize his time and be as efficient as possible. The fact that one person in this couple was so involved with social media while the other had a packed daily reality caused Paul to question his perceptions. In fact, he was correct, they were not on the same page; she was in cyberspace while he juggled reality on his own.

THERAPY: WORKING WITH FEARS THROUGH THE STRENGTHS PERSPECTIVE

The expectations and pressure that Judy felt distracted her from appreciating the positive aspects of Paul and enjoying the time they spent together. Judy was preoccupied with the messages she was receiving from social media, comparing her life with the so-called fabulous lives of others. On top of the demanding, competitive law school environment, Paul felt overwhelmed with the pressure he felt from Judy. He questioned his own feelings and ability to commit to a relationship, simply because he knew he wasn't ready to be engaged. He wondered if he was "supposed to feel ready" because that was the message he received from Judy.

I worked with Judy and Paul on rediscovering common ground in the relationship, reminding them why they were together and why they were committed to each other. I first asked Judy to express why she felt she loved Paul. She explained:

> Paul is an amazing guy. I love his passion and creativity. He pushes me to be better and to go outside my comfort zone. Besides being extremely attracted to him, he is my best friend and makes me feel comfortable to talk about anything. We also have a ton in common. We both love watching football, reading, and traveling.

Next, it was Paul's turn to talk about Judy:

> Judy is awesome. Obviously, I'm very attracted to her, but besides that, she is super smart. I appreciate her independence and she is just so lovable. I also agree with her that we have a ton in common. We both also value our families, which I think is important.

Their excitement and desire for one another was transparent. Their goals for the future matched up as well, with both Judy and Paul expressing interest in marriage, having a family, and moving to the suburbs. Judy and Paul's chemistry during the session was evident in their witty banter and endless displays of affection. When the topic of marriage was mentioned, we explored their underlying fears. Judy expressed her worry that Paul in some way didn't love her enough if he didn't want to get engaged. She explained how, when she sees those social media images of other couples, her insecurity skyrockets. She falsely assumed that Paul was ambivalent about his feeling toward her, when in actuality, Paul felt extremely confident about Judy and simply did not feel professionally and financially ready to move forward. Paul assured Judy that he saw that future with her but explained how it wasn't the right time.

Paul perceived that Judy wanted their relationship to progress more quickly. He explained to Judy during the session about how overwhelmed he was from school, how he felt behind his classmates intellectually, and how her overanalyzing was making him feel incompetent in their relationship. Judy listened and processed Paul's feelings in regard to marriage. She then explained to Paul that she was not necessarily eager to get engaged, but rather wanted to feel secure in the relationship. Judy's reaction to the couples on social media came across to Paul as not only her doubting his feelings toward her but also gave him the feeling that he needed to move the relationship to the next level or lose her. During therapy, Judy realized that her response to the social media posts was only a projection of her own insecurity that could be resolved by having an honest conversation with Paul.

THERAPY: REDUCING SOCIAL MEDIA PRESSURE

Social media was the driving force creating this underlying pressure in their relationship. I asked Judy to show Paul and me some of the images that were causing her to be anxious. She showed couples pronouncing their engagements, wedding pictures, and photos of pregnant women. I asked Paul to start questioning Judy about her thoughts regarding the photos.

Paul pointed to a picture of a couple's engagement: "What do you think about when you see this picture?"

Judy: "They seem extremely happy and excited to be engaged."

Paul: "Okay, that's true. So what makes you anxious about that?"

Judy: "That maybe we're behind in some way. That if it's not happening now for us that it will never happen."

Paul: "So, you're worried that I don't see this in our future?"

Judy: "Hmm . . . yeah, I guess, kind of. Like I have this illogical fear that if you don't want it now, you'll never want it."

Paul: "Well, I can tell you that I do see it with you and I'm sure it will be awesome when it comes. But just like this couple looks so happy in this picture, that's how happy I feel with you now. And when we do get to that step, I'll be happy then, too. We aren't them, though, and they aren't us. We're doing things at our own time and I am okay with that."

Judy: "Yeah. That makes sense. I guess my insecurity just says that it's me that you don't want and that the issue isn't timing."

Paul: "That's not the case. You're all I want."

This session was helpful for a variety of reasons. Judy was embarrassed to share the images, as she felt vulnerable and ashamed that they affected her in such a catastrophical way. Paul's support and empathy provided her with relief and encouragement. Paul gained a better understanding of her thought process.

Allowing Paul to lead the conversation showed them that they have the tools to communicate about this topic on their own. Paul was able to understand

Judy's underlying fears and to adequately address them. Judy received validation of Paul's desire for her, and Paul felt relieved that Judy did not necessarily want to rush an engagement.

We also discussed other tools to reduce Judy's stress. Judy agreed to abandon all forms of social media for a couple of weeks, and then we reassessed her level of anxiety. Judy expressed in the next session that she felt free and lighter. She was able to enjoy spending time with Paul without thinking as much about the future. She felt content with where they were in their relationship. Removing herself from social media also allowed her to focus more at work and to perform better.

RESEARCH: "FRIENDS" ON FACEBOOK

Researchers Hui-Tzu Grace Chou and Nicholas Edge conducted a study where they looked at Facebook use and how it impacted "people's perceptions of others' lives."[1] Questionnaires included items measuring amount of time spent on Facebook and the number of years belonging to Facebook. The participants were 425 undergraduate students from the University of Utah. They found that the longer people have used Facebook, the stronger was their belief that others were happier than themselves, and the less they agreed that life is fair.

These researchers also found that the more "friends" people connected with on Facebook whom they did not know personally, the stronger they believed others had better lives than they did. In other words, looking at happy pictures of others on Facebook gives people an impression that others are "always" happy and having good lives, as evident from these pictures of happy moments.

The results of the research also found "that the more time people spent going out with their friends, the less they agreed that others have better lives and are happier."[2] This means that when people have more offline interactions with their friends, they are less persuaded that others are happier than themselves. One reason for this phenomenon is that, in person, friends tend to find out more about each other's lives, both positive and negative. Instead of being exposed to the solely positive images on social media, you hear the reality of your friends' experiences.

RESEARCH: EXCESSIVE POSTING ON SOCIAL MEDIA

Albright College assistant professor of psychology Gwendolyn Seidman, with Albright alumna Amanda Havens, surveyed Facebook users in romantic relationships and found that those satisfied with their relationship are more likely to use Facebook to post couple photos and details of their relationship, as well as affectionate comments on their partner's wall.[3]

Individuals high in relationship contingent self-esteem (RCSE), an unhealthy form of self-esteem that depends on how well your relationship is going, are also more likely to post affectionate content.

However, these individuals also felt the need to brag about their relationship to others and even monitor their boyfriend or girlfriend's Facebook activities. For those high in RCSE, having something go wrong in the relationship is an even bigger blow to his or her self-esteem than it would be for someone low in RCSE, said Seidman. "These results suggest that those high in RCSE feel a need to show others, their partners and perhaps themselves that their relationship is 'OK' and, thus, they are OK," said Seidman.

According to the researchers, individuals high in neuroticism are also more likely to use Facebook to monitor their partner and show off their relationship. "This is what we expected, given that neurotic individuals are generally more jealous in their romantic relationships," said Seidman, who suggests these individuals may use Facebook as a way to lessen their fears of rejection and anxiety within the relationship.

What researchers did not expect is that extraverts, of whom past research has shown generally to have more Facebook friends and are more active users, are less likely to monitor their partners or make affectionate posts. Introverts, however, are more likely to post affectionate content and are more likely to snoop on their significant other.

SOCIAL MEDIA STALKING

Case Study: Sandy's Jealousy

Sandy, a 24-year-old female, barged into her session holding and waving her phone. Before I could calm her down, she yelled, "Who the f*** is that standing next to Brian? Is she kidding, with her hand on his thigh"? Sandy and Brian had gone on three dates and were not exclusive. The photo she showed me was Brian and a group of other young adults at a concert. Brian and a female were crouching in the front of the group. Brian had his arm around her shoulder, and her hand was resting on his thigh. Objectively, it appeared to be a photo of a group of friends at a concert. It may or may not have been Brian with a girlfriend. It was unclear exactly when the photo was taken. However, for Sandy, this photo was "clear proof" that he was "hooking up" with the girl in the photo.

ANALYSIS: SANDY'S PHOTO JEALOUSY

Sandy seemed overly concerned with the photo of Brian and this girl, given that she had dated him only three times and they had not talked about being in a monogamous relationship. From the outside, she may even sound slightly paranoid.

However, this is a common situation that occurs for both females and males. It is feasible that Brian was "hooking up" with the girl in the photo. After all, he and Sandy were free to see other people. On the other hand, he could have just been posing for a photo, enjoying the company of his female friend.

Facebook, Instagram, and Snapchat provide easy ways to impulsively stalk, or "accidently" view photos of the person you are casually dating. This can contribute to feelings of jealousy. Anyone can overanalyze photos with no context of the situation. A harmless photo of two people enjoying a day at the park can morph into an irrational thought that these two people are in love, having sex, or planning their future together.

It is difficult to avoid upsetting images, as they tend to pop up everywhere regardless of whom you block or unfollow. If you don't see images that were directly posted by your partner, it's possible that you see your partner in the background of Snapchats or posts of other people. No matter who posted the picture, Sandy's insecurity skyrocketed immediately upon seeing the photo. It didn't matter that they weren't exclusive. She felt jealous and personally targeted. Sandy did not feel she was at a point in the relationship to confront Brian about the picture. She wanted to maintain control and to appear cool, calm, and collected. So, instead of expressing her doubts and fear, she panicked internally.

Photography is an art that has transformed tremendously through digitalization and social media. In the past, it took effort (and cost) to develop film. These pictures were displayed in a photo album or in a frame on a coffee table. The pictures recaptured memories for the owner to reflect on or share with others. With the advent of Facebook, Instagram, and Snapchat, pictures are often taken spontaneously and posted impulsively. The subjects do not necessarily agree to have their picture taken, nor do they have control as to who sees the pictures, since they are posted by others. This phenomenon affects people differently. Some people don't care how they look, perhaps because there are so many photos that a few bad ones don't make a difference. For some, like Sandy, who may be experiencing loneliness or insecurity, photos are scrutinized and the analysis often includes a projection of inadequacy.

ANALYSIS: THE SOCIAL MEDIA EFFECT

Sandy liked Brian. She enjoyed spending time with him and was interested in pursuing their relationship further. This normal, typical thought process has always been around, even before technology existed. You like someone, you hope they like you back, and if the admiration is mutual, then the individuals venture on more dates to get to know each other better. However, as you can see in Sandy's case, social media affects this process. Prior to technology, what people did on their own time was much more private. If social media did not exist, Sandy would have had no idea that Brian was at that concert with a female friend, that is, unless he chose to tell her. Her anxiety about what he was doing on the side would be reduced significantly. Therefore, if she experienced any stress, it would be due to the nature of the relationship, not as a result of influences outside her control.

With social media, the private sphere is minimal. Eating with friends, going to the movies, and traveling are not only experiences simply enjoyed between friends. Now, we publicize those memories for all our social media friends to view. Therefore, in the dating world, it is possible that any picture you post or has been posted of you will be viewed by those you date. The constant connectedness creates additional triggers of jealousy, fear, and overanalyzing.

THERAPY SESSION: INTERVENTIONS FOR SANDY

Working with Sandy required a combination of mindfulness and cognitive behavioral therapy. The beauty of cognitive behavioral therapy (CBT) is that it is short term and goal oriented. Ideally, CBT enables people to alter the way they think and act and in doing so positively affects their feelings in response. People are able to gain control over their behavior, which helps them develop confidence in themselves and recognize the potential to change behaviors that interfere with their quality of life. Mindfulness is a technique that people can use to pay active attention to what is going on in the present. It encourages active, open awareness without judgment. When we are mindful, we can look at our thoughts and feelings and sit with them. Our behavior becomes more purposeful, consistent with our feelings, and goal directed. This increased consciousness ultimately allows for better appreciation of daily experiences.

Using the mindfulness approach, Sandy first learned how to breathe whenever she began feeling overwhelmed from the images on her phone. She conditioned herself to take five deep breaths as soon as she saw a disconcerting picture. Then she made a mental image of a stop sign in her mind, giving her the signal to slow down her thoughts. She practiced this multiple times in the therapy room. Sandy would show me photos of people that she casually dated or of ex-boyfriends that made her jealous. She would then put down her phone and attempt the breathing exercises.

Next, using CBT, she questioned her fears, using logic to analyze her concerns. She asked questions aloud, such as, "What do I really see in this photo?" "Am I jumping to irrational conclusions?" "What is the root of my jealousy?" We discussed the pictures in detail, and she responded to her own questions in order to process her thoughts. With exes, she reminded herself of why the relationship failed and how she ultimately wanted something and someone different. She also recognized that those pictures were not necessarily accurate representations of the couples' relationship. It is impossible to know what is happening behind closed doors, so to react with no context is illogical.

Additional strategies that I utilized included having Sandy spend less time on social media and more time strengthening her confidence and independence. She exercised more and made more plans with close friends. She focused on advancing her career and continued to date. Distracting herself with positive, healthy behaviors reduced her time spent scrolling social media and gave her more ease when she happened to skim a nerve-wracking photo.

RESEARCH: SOCIAL MEDIA AND JEALOUSY

Researchers Sonja Utz and Camiel Beukeboom studied both the positive and negative effects of using social networking sites on romantic relationships. They surveyed 56 males and 138 females at a Dutch university.[4] Participants were asked about their frequency of social media use, about why they used social media, and about their jealousy regarding their partner's social media use.

They found that low-self-esteem individuals experienced more SNS (social network sites) jealousy than high-self-esteem individuals did. For low self-esteem individuals, the need for popularity, trait jealousy, and monitoring behavior predicted SNS jealousy. For high-self-esteem individuals, monitoring behavior and SNS use for grooming were the main predictors of SNS jealousy.

Researchers Amy Muise, Emily Christofides, and Serge Desmarais conducted a study in which they predicted that time spent on Facebook would uniquely contribute to Facebook-specific jealousy beyond the effects of the personal and relational factors.[5]

> The open nature of Facebook gives people access to information about their partner that would not otherwise be accessible. The information listed on one's Facebook page may be interpreted in a variety of ways given its frequent lack of context. Real or imagined negative situations invoke feelings of jealousy, and participants felt the Facebook environment created these feelings and enhanced concerns about the quality of their relationship.[6]

Their results suggest that Facebook may expose an individual to potentially jealousy-provoking information about their partner. This can create a feedback loop where heightened jealousy leads to increased surveillance of a partner's Facebook page. Persistent surveillance results in further exposure to jealousy-provoking information.

RESEARCH: JEALOUSY AND SOCIAL MEDIA

Researcher Rianne Farrugia from the Rochester Institute of Technology conducted an online survey, in which 255 respondents provided information about their significant other and answered questions dealing with elements of relationship satisfaction, Facebook usage, surveillance, and jealousy. She hypothesized that with technology and the ease of partner monitoring online, one might begin to see a rise in jealousy between couples.

The results from this study found that as a relationship develops, so does surveillance of partners' Facebook pages. However, as the relationship progresses, Facebook usage decreases. Farrugia stated, "It is not surprising that individuals would check their partner's social media accounts to ensure and protect their relationship stability. The regression analysis illustrates that as a relationship matures, Facebook usage decreases. This means as couples get more intimate, they spend less time online."[7] This means that people in serious relationships are spending less time on social media; however, when they do decide to log onto Facebook, they are checking each other's pages.

She also found that couples who are on Facebook are likely to become more jealous when there is more information exposed to the public. Facebook usage correlates with jealousy because couples are trying to balance their current relationship in an online environment. Ultimately, she determined, as Facebook usage increased, the levels of jealousy felt also increased.[8]

It is understandable that partners who care about each other want to "check in" online, just as they do in person or via text. This is especially true when relationships are just starting to blossom. Individuals can see what their "crushes" are up to without directly contacting their partners. This type of cyberstalking can directly spark jealousy, which can be harmful to the relationship and anxiety provoking.

IMPLICATIONS FOR THERAPISTS

A client may present with feelings of anxiety, insecurity, jealousy, sadness or loneliness in response to being active on social media. Validating and normalizing those experiences are crucial in developing rapport with these clients, as expressing those feelings might lead to shame and embarrassment. The Facebook Intrusion Questionnaire is an example of how to better evaluate your client's emotional response to social media usage. You can work with your client to identify what visuals on social media may trigger negative emotions, and explore their visceral responses.

ASSESSMENT QUESTIONNAIRE

Therapists are often in the position of assessing clients. There are scales available to provide assessments of symptoms of depression (e.g., Phq9), anxiety (e.g., GAD7), alcohol (e.g., AUDIT), and drug use (e.g., DAST.) These measures, which are self-reported, enable clinicians to judge more objectively

Items

1. I often think about Facebook when I am not using it (cognitive salience)
2. I often use Facebook for no particular reason (behavioral salience)
3. Arguments have arisen with others because of my Facebook use (interpersonal conflict)
4. I interrupt whatever else I am doing when I feel the need to access Facebook (conflict with other activities)
5. I feel connected to others when I use Facebook (euphoria)
6. I lose track of how much I am using Facebook (loss of control)
7. The thought of not being able to access Facebook makes me feel distressed (withdrawal)
8. I have been unable to reduce my Facebook use (relapse and reinstatement)

Figure 5.1 Facebook Intrusion Questionnaire. (Rachel A. Elphinston and Patricia Noller, "Time to Face It! Facebook Intrusion and the Implications for Romantic Jealousy and Relationship Satisfaction," *Cyberpsychology, Behavior, and Social Networking* 14, no. 11 (May 2011): 631–635, doi:10.1089/cyber.2010.0318. Used by permission of Mary Ann Liebert, Inc. via Copyright Clearance Center)

how clients perceive these issues to be impacting their daily lives. The self-assessments could be used once as a baseline, or more frequently, to determine whether intervention was successful in promoting change. Similarly, the Facebook Intrusion Questionnaire, developed by researchers Rachel Elphinston and Patricia Noller, is based on key features of technological (behavioral) addictions.[9] The Facebook Intrusion Questionnaire is an eight-item device with a single-factor structure.

This questionnaire is a great starting point to spark a conversation with a client regarding Facebook behavior. I appreciate how Elphinston and Noller specifically outline what each item is expected to measure. Responses are reported on a 7-point scale. Not all items have to be used in a therapy session, but it is an interesting approach to gather information from clients on how Facebook is affecting them physically and emotionally.

Being self-aware of your comfort level in discussing social media is as important as knowing your personal triggers. There is no point in reinventing the wheel, especially in a topic that seems foreign. Therefore, using questionnaires that are already in existence will provide you with the language to broach an unfamiliar topic.

USING THE STRENGTH PERSPECTIVE

As the preceding research showed, having low self-esteem can directly correlate with feelings of jealousy around a partner's use of social media. Highlighting a client's strengths is a typical technique used in all types of therapy. Whatever the diagnosis, using a client's strengths to overcome or cope with the issue is helpful for treatment. If a client is affected by social media to the degree that he or she becomes anxious, overwhelmed, or insecure, then using the strength perspective is especially helpful. Part of the technique in assisting clients who struggle with social media is to increase independence and self-worth. For example, with Sandy, we focused on her strengths in exercising, in her career, and in her support network. Once Sandy discovered and then built on her strengths, she was less inclined to check social media and to be affected by certain photos that previously caused her discomfort.

UTILIZING SELF-AWARENESS

When you see a photo, your subconscious creates these irrational thoughts as described earlier. Without further information, it is impossible to fully understand the context of the photo and, therefore, your mind runs wild with possibilities. Understanding this phenomenon and becoming self-aware is the first step in taking control of your reaction.

Remind yourself that what you are seeing is what the individuals in the photo *want* you to see. It is not satisfying to post pictures of depression, heartbreak, or loss. No one wants to brag about their failures. So in essence, you are seeing a skewed picture of someone's life, with major elements removed. Taking a step back to recognize your own feelings in response to the photo can help you recognize your own fears and concerns. You can engage in self-talk and remind yourself that the photos you see are not a full representation of a person's life. Every relationship has its own sets of problems, and every person has issues to tackle in life. Instead of comparing, remind yourself of your personal strengths and the real connections you have that bring you happiness.

SUMMARY

We are living in a new era of information overload, which encompasses a concern for privacy because our activity is tracked and used for advertisement purposes. Amazon knows what type of dress we were seeking, Facebook knows for whom we are searching, and advertisements pop up incessantly, targeting our specific interests. Besides the influx of product descriptions, we are also faced with knowing what an inordinate number of people are doing at any given point of time. The constant stimulation of the brain can be exhausting. Sometimes we need to take a moment to breathe and relax.

The desire to post, read posts, and be connected is part of human nature. The act of posting can be entertaining and amusing. You can share memories and experiences and receive feedback, support, and validation almost immediately. Many people feel that connecting on social media is a way to expel the feeling of loneliness. Social media can be a positive way to keep in touch with friends and to retain memories. It can also be an entertaining, enjoyable experience where you can share with others what is occurring in your life.

The key is to be mindful about what you are posting and why. Are you posting to share the moment with friends, in order to feel like they were a part of the experience? Do you welcome the feeling of an expanded social network that encompasses more than the people living in close proximity? Or are you disappointed with the responses of those you are physically with and need more of an acknowledgment?

Additionally, try paying attention to your reaction when you see others' posts. If you find yourself feeling anxious, insecure, jealous, or angry, take a moment and be mindful of those emotions. Try to determine the root of the projection. If you feel positive emotions, such as confidence, joy, or excitement, it is also worthwhile to sit with that response. Being supported by friends, even through social media, can contribute to your own well-being. These shared experiences can enable friends and family to maintain closeness. Ultimately, your use of social media and your reactions to posts can help enlighten you about how you truly feel about yourself and your life. Similar to all use of technology, we have the capacity to control our attitude toward the experience. Red flags should go up for you if social media begins to become a source of negativity rather than a catalyst of fun.

Chapter 6

DATING APPS AND THE SWIPING PHENOMENON

I am going to preface this chapter by stating that it contains more personal stories than any other chapter. When I first constructed the outline for this book, I knew a chapter on dating apps was necessary. However, I was honest with myself that I was certainly not an expert on dating apps. I conducted research to explore and subsequently convey the complexity of the dating app phenomenon. The goal was to obtain and analyze diverse perspectives on this growing trend that affects how people meet, date, and interact on a daily basis.

The overwhelmed and confusing feelings that emerged for me while collecting this data parallel the real concerns of dating app members. It is nearly impossible to come to a concise conclusion in regard to dating apps, but I believe that is the quintessential point. Like all other tech products, they are in a state of continual development. They are here to stay and will grow, progress, and become more technologically advanced.

According to a Pew Research Center survey conducted in 2016, nearly half of the public knows someone who uses online dating or has met a spouse or partner via online dating. The share of 18- to 24-year-olds who use online dating has roughly tripled from 10 percent in 2013 to 27 percent today (2017). Online dating use among 55- to 64-year-olds has also risen substantially since the last Pew Research Center survey on the topic. Today, 12 percent of 55- to 64-year-olds report using an online dating site or mobile dating app versus only 6 percent in 2013.[1]

So, it is clear that dating apps are being downloaded. But who are the users and what are their intentions? Although the percentage of individuals using dating apps have significantly increased, around one-third of people who have used online dating *have never actually gone on a date with someone they met on these sites.* It proves the idea that there is not just one motive for joining a dating app. To gain more clarity, I set up focus groups with dating app users between 23 and 31 years of age. The participants in my focus groups painted a clearer picture of this wild, growing phenomenon.

Following is the breakdown of my data. Don't worry, along the way, I will share tips and tools for applying this data to your own dating life or your work with clients. This new dating process also introduces new language. To comprehend dating apps and how they work, you need to grasp some of the lingo. Here are terms and definitions that came up during the interviews.

> **Swipe left**: When you literally swipe left on someone's profile, which indicates you are not interested in connecting.
>
> **Swipe right**: Alternatively, when you are somewhat interested, you can swipe right on someone's profile.
>
> **Match**: When both people swipe right on each other's profile, they become a match and can begin to communicate through the app.
>
> **Meet cute**: When a couple meets for the first time in a way that is considered adorable, entertaining, or amusing (it is used specifically to describe a face-to-face meeting rather than online).

I thought it best to start with a dating app story as told by one participant in the focus group: Lisbeth, a 26-year-old psychologist living in New York City. She shared her narrative with the other focus group members: Sarah, a 26-year-old project manager, and Ashley, a 26-year-old advertising professional. All names have been changed for confidentiality.

NARRATIVE: LISBETH'S DATING DISASTER

Lisbeth: I went on dating app, JSwipe, Jews in Search of Jews, and I matched with someone who was on a dating site! So obviously, my first expectation is that you're single. Because [pause] you are on a dating site. He was Israeli, really good-looking, tall, had a beard. I thought the stars were aligned. He was everything I could've wanted and more. So he messaged me and we were chatting. Great ratio of chat to date. Very little chatter and more of "Let's meet up." He told me he was between Israel and New York for work. He was some sort of journalist. So he was here for two weeks and we went on dates. Not ordinary dates, but really lavish dates. He even took me to a Broadway show and then we went for drinks after. Two nights later, we went for a nice dinner!

Sarah: Looking back, do you think those lavish dinners could've been red flags? However, I agree that when you match with someone on a dating app, you assume they are single.

> **Ashley:** I wouldn't think so. I think we don't understand being taken out by someone who's wealthy like that. Not like the 27-year-olds we date.
>
> **Lisbeth:** Yeah. It was nice doing something different. Plus, he's not really from here so I felt that he wanted to do all the New York cultural stuff. Made sense to me. Plus, it felt good that he didn't want to take any of the other hundred girls on JSwipe touring around. He wanted to take me! So I put on Broadway's best and we went to see *Mamma Mia*. Halfway through the production, he held my hand and I thought, "This is nice. This is what I'm going to tell my grandchildren." I knew he was only here for two weeks and he did everything to see me. Sent pictures of himself from his business events, took cabs to my apartment right after, so it really felt like an intense two-week relationship.

When I told my Israeli coworker that I had met an Israeli journalist, we decided to cyberstalk him. In one of the videos on YouTube, he was wearing a wedding ring, which was weird. My friend tried to assure me and said maybe he was married and now he's divorced, the video was from two or three years earlier. So I brought it up with him and he said it was a ring that his father gave him and it sounded plausible to me!

We continued stalking in future days at work, because I couldn't think about anything else besides my Israeli lover. We stumbled upon a documentary. It was all in Hebrew about him, his wife, and kids and I thought, "Gotcha!" I brought it up to him and he still denied it! It got to the point where he said the producers thought it would be better for his image to be married with kids. And he stuck to it until the end. Denied, denied, denied until the end. After that, he basically just stopped answering me.

WHY DO PEOPLE JOIN DATING APPS?

At first, you would think the reason people join dating apps is obviously to date, right? Wrong. Some people do, for sure. But if I learned anything from these focus group participants, there are countless reasons someone might decide to download and chat on a dating app. The uncertainty of why someone might be chatting with you can lead to confusion and frustration. But without further ado, let's hear the reasons these participants joined the trend.

> **Sarah** [heterosexual, female, 26, New York]: I avoided dating apps because of the stigma. I kinda liked the idea of meeting someone walking outside or at a bar. This is the wrong word, but I didn't feel desperate enough. Then, at some point, I decided that I really want to meet someone. I noticed everyone is going on dates, why shouldn't I?
>
> **Lisbeth** [heterosexual, female, 26, New York]: Our friends go out with the same people all the time, so I'm not meeting new people. People at bars are just drunk and wasted and are not trying to have a real connection. Basically, it doesn't seem like there is any other option.

Joe   [heterosexual, male, 26, New York]: So I lived in Boston for three and a half years and I was like, "I'm never gonna use my app." I was not meeting people anywhere and finally tried Tinder. It put me in the mind-set of getting out there more. I was just not in a good place mentally and I didn't know what else to do. Like, what are my other options? It's a "necessary evil." These fairytale stories . . . people say they want them but they don't actually try and it's only getting worse.

Ben   [heterosexual, male, 29, New York]: Meet people to have sex with . . . quickly.

James   [gay, male, 27, Denver]: I joined mostly to see if there were other gay guys around me. I remember opening Grindr when I was younger and looking to see if I knew anyone on there, to see if there was anyone else in the same boat as me that I knew. I also remember going on Tinder and switching it from girls to guys to see if I saw anyone I knew. I quickly changed it back to girls. I didn't have any pressure to join. I joined mostly because I wanted to see who else was gay and if there were any gay guys I knew.

Max   [gay, male, 28, New York]: Occasionally I use them to find other people. I am in a long-term relationship, but we use it to find other people to have sex with, but not too regularly.

Richard [gay, male, 30, Berlin]: When I am slightly intoxicated and want to sleep with someone.

Marissa [lesbian, female, 28, New York]: I initially joined apps because the dating pool due to preferences was extremely small. There were no real options "to be set up" by a friend. I didn't feel any type of pressure, but I was interested in dating and it seemed like the best way to find what I was looking for without having to go to gay bars, which is not my scene, or go through other people, which can get awkward.

Mark   [gay, male, 28, New York]: As a shy person with anxiety tendencies but also as a gay male, I'm never entirely comfortable approaching someone in public. For the extreme rejection you can experience. That you can offend someone or someone is going to be aggressive or repulsed. It's just hard to know who is gay and who isn't. So apps just smooth that process.

Greg   [heterosexual, male, 31, New York]: I was looking to find someone, having trouble finding potential mates and meeting people in the real world. There was some pressure to join from some friends and family, but nothing unbearable.

WHICH APPS DO PEOPLE JOIN AND WHY?

Obviously people join dating apps for a variety of reasons. Some people are just looking for sex, while others are looking for long-term relationships. Participants also noted that they use the apps to just chat when they are lonely. When I started writing this book, my assumption was that there were just a few choices of apps to join, along with paying websites like JDate and Christian Mingle. Wow, was I wrong! The competition to create "the best app" is still out there, and the choices are limitless. It forced me to ponder why adults are choosing certain apps over others.

Amanda   [heterosexual, female, 26, New York]: The League, Hinge, and Bumble. I like the ability to filter for religion. Bumble is a bit frustrating because of that. If you don't know if someone is going to meet your religious criteria, it's not worth it to reach out.

Michael   [heterosexual, male, 27, New York]: Bumble has always been least successful for me. Common male theory. Bumble is designed to show you the ten hottest girls in the world. It's the first girls they show you so it keeps you on it but you never actually match with them. When you do get a match, it's that one ugly girl that you didn't even mean to say yes to.

Mark   [gay, male, 28, New York]: Scruff and Grindr . . . I have used Tinder in the past, and OKCupid, but primarily Scruff because of demographics and also I find that the interface and the way it allows you to interact is better. Scruff is a location-based grid so you can see who is immediately there and there's more photo sharing capabilities and more space to fill out to write about yourself, so I just feel a little bit more informed about the person I'm dating.

Greg   [heterosexual, male, 31, New York]: Coffee Meets Bagel seemed friendlier because there was less of a pressure to just match and connect all the time, because of the one-per-day message feature.

Stacey   [heterosexual, female, 31, New York]: I liked Coffee Meets Bagel because of the texting feature. I think if someone is willing to text you for a week, they have more invested and are looking for more than a hook-up. Also allows better screening.

I began to recognize from conducting research that many apps actually have unique features targeting specific audiences. Apps exist to find other people who meditate, to help you meet up with someone for a specific activity, to match you with someone with similar taste in music, and so much more. I think about the future of dating apps and imagine the next trend. Will there be one app that dominates and controls the entire industry? It seems that despite a crowded app market, people are continuously launching new dating apps to appeal to a specific population.

WHEN DO YOU SWIPE?

Now that you've downloaded a bunch of apps, it's time to review your matches. But when? I was curious to hear when people decide to pull out their phones and swipe. Is there an ideal time during the day or season of the year to review the profiles of people you've matched with?

Amanda   [heterosexual, female, 26, New York]: The scrolling is part of the compulsive nature of apps. It's very mindless. I have found myself, at times, endlessly scrolling and not even paying attention. It's almost like a nervous habit like the way you scroll through Instagram or Facebook. So maybe I'm out and I want to meet someone but I pull out my phone and scroll out of habit, like a reflex.

Joe	[heterosexual, male, 26, New York]: When I need validation. When a hot girl swipes for me I am like F*** yes. That one second is amazing. It's like an addiction. The dopamine is certainly released when I get a match.
Michael	[heterosexual, male, 27, New York]: It revolves around when I'm getting laid. In the summer, there are more opportunities because I'm out more and around more than during the winter when it's 25 degrees and I don't want to go out. So my sex life isn't going great. I also swipe when I'm not doing stuff or don't want to be doing stuff. If I were laying here chillin' and I'm high and my roommates are watching a show I don't love, I'm gonna open Facebook, Instagram, and see if there are any girls I can match with . . . our brains are always looking for something to do.
Ben	[heterosexual, male, 29, New York]: When I have WiFi.
Richard	[gay, male, 30, Berlin]: When I'm drunk.
Lauren	[heterosexual, female, 29, New York]: At night before I go to bed. But mostly because I've found them to be disappointing. If they were higher quality, I might be on them all day.

It seemed like the consensus was to swipe when bored or as a distraction. Many people swipe at night after work, while lying in bed. A bedroom is a very intimate place. It makes sense that people swipe to find a partner to sleep with or to date when they are located in a place of intimacy. Perhaps the loneliness makes them take that step.

WHAT DO YOU LOOK FOR IN A PROFILE?

So you're swiping and swiping, intentionally or aimlessly, but lo and behold, someone catches your eye. What is it? What's in their picture? Is there something specific in their profile that makes you take a second look?

Stephanie	[heterosexual, female, 28, New York]: On a really superficial level, I only like facial hair, so if you don't have facial hair, I won't match with you . . . There are some apps that you can filter for that.
Lauren	[heterosexual, female, 29, New York]: Jewish. Height. Profession, I have to see that they are driven. Or a runner, something I like to do. It sucks because those are shallow things, but there is no other option.
Michael	[heterosexual, male, 27, New York]: I hate when girls say "I'm looking for an adventure . . . you are not an adventurer because you went to the West Village and had brunch . . . it bothers me . . . It's also a problem when it's four pictures in and you haven't showed your face . . . also travel. Cool, you like to go on vacations. Who doesn't?"
Marissa	[lesbian, female, 28, New York]: Unfortunately, dating apps do reveal a shallow aspect of judging people based on their looks. However, on Hinge, I did look at our friend connections, their school, and if they showed where they were working. Anyone with selfies I pretty much always swiped left for or anyone that seemed to be hiding their face/body in a lot of them.

I liked seeing profiles with a range of pictures: friends, family, alone (but not a selfie, doing activities, etc.)

James   [gay, male, 27, Denver]: Commonalities with personal interests/education level. Pictures with friends, face pictures that someone else took, aka not selfies with that goddamn dog filter. Oh, and by the way, it seems like all feminine-acting bottoms use the same filters—the flower one or the dog one. It's a good way to let people know you like to be dominated. Just a little tidbit from the gay world.

Stacey   [heterosexual, female, 31, New York]: I was looking for a Jew with a good job. Also was looking for someone who seemed fun and didn't take themselves too seriously. I didn't appreciate people who seemed to be fake in their profiles. Over 5'7" was also important.

The common theme is that it is hard to get a realistic portrayal of someone from his or her profile. You also have to trust that the pictures they show and the information they provide is accurate. What I gathered is that members want to see what's real and not be fooled. If they think they are being fooled because you are only uploading group photos or face pictures, they will tend to swipe left. Those individuals looking for something more serious look more into the facts in the profile because occupation and/or interests matter. If the end goal is sex, then the images are more significant.

According to one research study, 60 percent of online daters lie about their weight, 48 percent about their height, and 19 percent about their age.[2] Additionally, photos associated with the longest conversations include those depicting travel, animals, or an interesting activity. Women do better when they give a flirty look at the camera and men do better when they look away and don't smile.

The ability to create an online profile allows people to create a version of themselves they want to display. They want to put out their best pictures or write a witty bio that will draw people to match with them. If the goal is just to get that match validation, then this works in their favor. However, if you are looking to form a real connection and relationship, then eventually the real you will show. It is fascinating to me when people get help from third-party companies to create their profiles or write messages for them. Some people enlist friends to take over their accounts. I understand asking for help, but in the end, only you, your personality, and your appearance will matter.

HOW LONG DO YOU TYPICALLY CHAT WITH SOMEONE ON AN APP?

So you made the decision to join an app, selected a few specific ones to download, and made a few matches. Now comes the easy part, right? You match and get a date. Not exactly. Because as I've learned, not everyone on these apps is so eager to jump into dating. Let's hear from a few of the participants about the proper chat-to-date ratio.

Ashley   [heterosexual, female, 27, New York]: The reason I started to hate dating apps is because of this f***** up, stupid small-talk thing you have to do to get a date, which is annoying because you have to be funny but also you don't know the person so personally. Basically, my jokes don't land. It's hard to impress someone. But if you give up on that and say "Hey, what's up," you get like, "Lame! You couldn't think of anything better than that?" There is no winning. I would like to know the girls who are winning and what are they saying. Then you have a basic conversation about nothing. If you have three conversation topics and don't get into the "let's go on a date," then I move on. It makes me angry to have all this small talk without meeting up.

Sarah   [heterosexual, female, 26, New York]: People are just not on them for the same reason. Some people just want to chat on them just to like keep their game up. Some people also have more anxiety about it so they just chat but are too nervous to ask someone out. It's impossible to know their intention even when they are on an app.

Michael   [heterosexual, male, 27, New York]: Sometimes I just chat with a girl cause I'm bored and other times they just stop chatting with me. I'll go typically five back-and-forths before we go on a date. I always call before going on a date. It's a power move. From the phone call, I can also decide if I'm actually into them.

James   [gay, male, 27, Denver]: I used to talk to people for like months before meeting them, but that was kind of the life of a young gay not feeling comfortable with himself yet. Every gay guy I know "fell in love" with a guy on Tinder before ever meeting them. You definitely crave the physical part when you first come out and try dating the same sex. However, even moreso, for me, was the need for the emotional connection that was missing in my current relationships. I talked with this one guy, Pat, for three months and literally loved him, but we never even met. So ridiculous, in retrospect. Now I don't have the energy, so I ask people for drinks pretty quickly. A day or two.

Richard   [gay, male, 30, Berlin]: I never want to have a conversation that lasts more than ten lines. I wanna say, "Hey, this is great, let's go get a drink." So if a conversation is not progressing then I would quickly move on. If people want to engage in too much chat then I don't have time.

It was interesting to see the participants converse with each other in response to this question. There were such varying perspectives based on two main ideas. Individuals will vary their chat length on an app based on the reason they joined the app in the first place. If they are chatting out of boredom, it is likely those will continue for a lengthier period of time with no aim to ever meet. If their goal is to have sex, then the chat is minimal because having a physical interaction is the objective. There were varying ideas about what to do if the intention is to find a relationship. Some participants felt strongly about vetting partners first, while others wanted a brief back-and-forth before engaging in a face-to-face date. Many of the male participants mentioned the struggle with finances in regard to dating apps. They were more skeptical of initiating a date right away because they did know they would be spending a significant amount of money. They wanted to be more secure with their interest before investing their time and money.

The second theme that emerged was trial and error. Based on individual experiences, participants changed their tactics regarding time spent chatting. Success rates determined whether individuals would continue lengthy discussions prior to meeting or if they would change their habits. The focus groups demonstrated how open the individuals were to changing their techniques regarding dating apps. They picked up ideas from each other and were willing to adapt in order to reach their ideal goal.

HOW DO YOU HANDLE THE OVERFLOW OF CHOICES?

The theory of paradox of choice is a topic I cover substantially in another chapter. The focus group participants all acknowledged that it certainly affects modern dating. Always having another match at your fingertips can be addicting and may cause "the grass is always greener" mentality. This is not something that only happens to those on dating apps, but having more choices so easily accessible can be daunting. I decided to bring up this idea, to further explore how dating apps could potentially cause or exacerbate this mind-set.

Lisbeth   [heterosexual, female, 26, New York]: Dating apps are so instant and immediate that when I go on a date, I won't really give them a fair chance because I can just take out my phone. If I met someone organically, I think I would be more committed.

Amanda   [heterosexual, female, 26, New York]: I'm a very big proponent of reducing my anxiety by keeping my options open. I do this by chatting with guys on the side even when I am seeing someone fairly consistently. So I wouldn't stop scrolling until I'm exclusively seeing someone. There's no point in not dating other people. I also am quick to feel anxious so it's important to feel more control and power so I will just keep dating people. . . . I started dating someone and he brought up not using the apps anymore and not wanting me to, so I deleted mine but it makes me anxious. It's not like I'm SO excited about this relationship that I'm dying to stop using the apps. I think the apps put you in a situation to make you think there's always someone else out there. I'm fearful of getting into another relationship so I want to make sure they are exactly what I'm looking for, so deleting the apps is scary.

Lauren   [heterosexual, female, 27, New York]: If I go on one good first date. On the way home, I might be on an app. If I do really like someone after two or three times, I'm very quick to stop because it's not like I love being on the apps. But also there is a vulnerability of stopping so I wouldn't be so quick to be all in with someone.

Michael [heterosexual, male, 27, New York]: Totally f***s up the dating experience. I think every single person sitting on a date is thinking, "I wonder what else is out there." I wonder if I go back on Bumble, if there'll be someone better. I think that girls are looking for free s*** sometimes. I know girls that accept a date for dinner and then another for drinks after. But for me, I would never spend money and date two girls the same night.

Max [gay, male, 28, New York]: I don't think I have that problem because I use it sparingly and for a particular purpose. It's pretty straightforward: I want that one.

Mark [gay, male, 28, New York]: I am concerned that I am falling into that camp that there is always something better out there. But I also don't think that's attributable to the apps but also living in a populated, transient place. But a sort of positive spin on it is that I'm a nervous, shy person so you would think that going on a first date would freak me out. But I've had so many opportunities and there's not as much urgency to get it perfect because there are others out there. So it has made dating a little less scary for me. So there are pros and cons.

Richard [gay, male, 30, Berlin]: This concept makes me cry sometimes.

Again, I don't believe that the apps themselves are the direct cause of the paradox of choice mind-set. Especially because people who don't use them can share that mentality. What is clear is that apps provide easier access to the "other options." It can potentially cause skepticism when you would typically feel more confident. This is not inherently harmful since, as I previously stated, choices may lead to finding a more suitable partner instead of settling.

DO YOU FEEL STIGMATIZED BEING A DATING APP USER?

How open are people to sharing that they are app users? How easy is it to disclose that you met and are dating someone you met through an app? Is this something that is so mainstream it feels the same as disclosing you met someone in a face-to-face situation?

Ashley [heterosexual, female, 27, New York]: I think it takes away this dream that it's gonna be this romantic *meet cute* meeting. It's not embarrassing; it's where we are today. But you think about that moment where your children and grandchildren ask you how you met your husband, and you want to be able to tell them a great story, and meeting on an app is not a great story. There's this Hollywood meeting . . . romantic meeting . . . that goes away in my head.

Stephanie [heterosexual, female, 27, New York]: I didn't think I would care but, in that moment when my boyfriend's friends asked how we met, I totally deferred to him, and he was like, "You want me to lie? We met on the

Internet." In the moment, I was so nervous but I was surprised by it. But I guess because there still is a bit of a stigma, even though there is such a huge percentage of people who get married from these apps.

Michael   [heterosexual, male, 27, New York]: At this point, no, because dating apps are so mainstream and I bet nine out of ten of my friends are on them. Five years ago, if I knew of someone who was on Match.com or something more serious, I would have laughed at it, but now it's so mainstream.

Ben   [heterosexual, male, 29, New York]: Both my parents are on dating websites so . . . I think it's just natural.

Marissa   [lesbian, female, 28, New York]: That seemed to be the case at first, but not anymore. Personally, I feel like more people know about apps and how widely used they are that it's becoming much more normal. Additionally, apps have changed a lot and people seem to be using them far less for just random hookups so that reputation is fading a bit. When explaining to "adults," it's a bit more awkward since they don't really get it, so we just say we met in the city.

Greg   [heterosexual, male, 31, New York]: My preconceived notions about apps were mostly negative—only losers were on dating apps, people on the apps were lying about themselves, etc. I was also afraid of being made fun of by friends/family who found my profile on the site.

SUMMARY OF FINDINGS

I recognize that I only interviewed individuals in their late 20s/early 30s and mostly those living in New York. These experiences may vary across age groups, regions, cultures, ethnicities, religions, and nationalities. However, as you can gather from my data, no two people had the exact same perspective across the board on their approach to successfully utilizing dating apps.

Dating apps provide immediate gratification. That gratification can be sex, a match, or simply an answer to boredom. As Joe explained, there is a dopamine release when one receives a match. It is a validation of worth and may increase confidence. Conversely, receiving no matches or having no match to initiate a conversation can be a blow to one's self-esteem.

I asked participants whether they would add anything to apps to help improve their chances of finding success. Some participants wanted apps to better transmit personality, since the common consensus was that apps are naturally superficial. Others suggested adding voice or somehow exchanging pheromones (not sure how that one is possible). One participant would prefer learning first about someone's values through an app. For example, she suggested posting scenarios and learning how people would react to those situations. There was an overwhelming request for meetups through an app, which some apps have already started. This would help create this natural *meet cute* moment that people are searching for.

It was clear that app dating is becoming increasingly mainstream. Most of the participants indicated that, in the past, they would have felt shame meeting someone through an app, but now feel more comfortable disclosing that they are app users. The app dating experience is also not something that the participants yearned for. Most felt there was a lack of options to meet people, but would prefer meeting organically, as opposed to an app.

UPDATE ON PARTICIPANTS

A few of the participants in these studies ended up finding relationships through the dating apps. I thought it was important to disclose these success stories, to show the value in the apps despite the frustration and skepticism voiced during the interviews.

Sarah met her current boyfriend through JSwipe. He actually messaged her a year prior to their first meeting. He said something and she didn't answer, as she thought his message was unoriginal. After a year, they matched again. When you go to message someone that you've previously messaged, your old messages pop up. So he saw his prior unanswered message and felt pressured to say something to spark her attention. She ended up answering him, and now they have been dating for several months.

Lisbeth is also dating someone she met through JSwipe. And he's Israeli.

Stephanie is dating someone she met through the League. She did delete the apps and was able to focus on her partner.

Ashley ended up having her fairytale story. Her long-term friend confessed that he wanted to date her and could not hold back his feelings. She felt similarly and they are now happily dating.

Lauren is still looking for love but is open-minded and continues to use dating apps.

Amanda is moving back to Chicago and is hoping that she will have better luck there finding love.

Greg and Stacey are currently married after meeting on Coffee Meets Bagel. They represent a real success story after meeting on an app. Both indicated their intention of going on the app was to find a serious relationship. They do not feel stigmatized from meeting through an app and are just happy they found each other.

IMPLICATIONS FOR THERAPISTS

According to a study conducted in 2016 by Trent Petrie and Jessica Strübel of the University of North Texas, Tinder users reported having lower levels of satisfaction with their faces and bodies and having lower levels of self-worth than the men and women who did not use Tinder.[3] The researchers found that being actively involved with Tinder, regardless of the user's gender, was associated with body dissatisfaction, body shame, body monitoring, internalization of societal expectations of beauty, comparing oneself physically to others, and reliance on media for information on appearance and attractiveness.

It is beneficial for a therapist to ask their clients questions on what rejection through an app means to them and if it's similar to other types of rejection. These questions will help spark a conversation relating to body image and self-worth. The apps can be a trigger for unveiling a range of negative or positive self-perceptions.

Exploring the rationale as to why clients are on a dating app and their motivation for choosing specific apps can be useful for understanding what the client is going through. Having a client describe her profile is a good indication of how she perceives her ideal self as differentiated from her real self.

Dating apps can be a successful tool in expanding a social network. I find from my clients that those who utilize dating apps as part of their overall objective to meet new people tend to do better than those who see it as "the means" to meet others. I have had some clients successfully meet people with whom they eventually married. These people tended to be more aware of important qualities and were at a point of honesty about themselves.

RECOGNIZING THE REWARD

It is clear there are varied reasons for joining a dating app. Part of treatment can include helping your client be mindful of their intentions. Amanda stated that being on dating apps reduced the overall level of her anxiety she experienced trying to find a partner. She identified her fear of losing control by being committed to one person. Dating apps diminished Amanda's sense of vulnerability. She was able to disperse her focus on various options without needing to feel pressured to choose one person. Her app behavior tells a story of her internal stressors and worries.

Michael described a mindless swiping behavior, which is a result of the gratification of unpredictable reinforcement. Like gambling, the unpredictable nature of a variable-ratio schedule can lead to a high frequency of behavior, as the animal (or human) may believe that the next press will "be the one" that delivers the reward. In layman's terms, if Michael keeps swiping, then perhaps the next swipe will yield him a reward (sex or something more).

Joe sought validation. Therapy would enable Joe to explore why his self-worth is tied to the match itself. Is matching with a woman the only way for him to feel attractive?

The therapist can help the client visualize his ideal scenario from joining an app. The client will have to be honest about his intention. Sometimes it is easier for clients to describe looking for something casual because there is less of a risk of failure. However, if the client is honest about his end goal, the therapist can help explore the values and characteristics that the client is looking for.

BEST ADVICE FOR USING DATING APPS

Dating apps can be an extremely useful way to meet people but can also have negative side effects. The best advice is to use the apps mindfully. Prior to swiping, ask yourself what you are looking for. If you are unsure, meet with a therapist to figure out your real intention. If you desire a relationship, think about the values you require in a partner.

Choosing a dating app that is geared toward your interests and meets your requirements can be a process. Apps have been developed for individuals who are older than 60, for individuals who enjoy meditating and outdoor activities, and for individuals with specific religious preferences. Ascertain the needs and priorities that are requirements for your happiness. Then choose an app accordingly.

Apply mindfulness to the act of swiping, as well. It is easy to get caught up and addicted to the swiping behavior. However, to find success on the apps, you should actually pay attention to the type of person you are seeking and allow for some flexibility of characteristics. At the end of the day, you are not swiping for a sandwich, but for a real-life human being.

SUMMARY

Many people find that dating apps are easier to use than matchmaking services, although both address the issue of expanding a social network. Motivations vary from being a fun activity with the hope of meeting new people to a more serious approach on a mission to find a soul mate. Hearing the real-life stories of people in my focus groups enabled me to learn about some of the different perspectives. Although I am aware that the responses described here are far from statistically relevant given the ages and the demographics, they do provide some significant insights. People in their 30s, 40s, 50s, 60s, 70s, and even 80s are on dating apps, and surveying their motivations and attitudes for using these apps would be fascinating (maybe for my next book). However, I believe we can safely concur that users' incentives to download and communicate through an app vary greatly. The attitudes of the users and the resulting process of maneuvering dating apps also fluctuate based on their personal goals. It will be interesting to see the future designs of dating apps and how virtual reality may play a vital role.

Chapter 7

SEXTING

CASE STUDY: LAURA'S LONG-DISTANCE LOVE INTEREST

Laura, a 27-year-old female, was dancing at a bar with her friends to 1990s show tunes. Once Backstreet Boys came on, they couldn't help but go wild. Laura laughed as she observed her friends singing, jumping, and fist pumping. However, in the back of her mind, she couldn't help but think about Madison, the woman she'd met on her 10-day vacation to Australia. She thought back to their passionate and erotic dancing at that nightclub in Sydney. Although she only spent a few days with Madison, she couldn't get the memory of her touch out of her head. She had never experienced such sensations. There was something about being erotic in public that appealed to Laura. As she danced with her friends, the flashbacks of Madison's touch consumed her thoughts. She turned to her friends and told them she was heading to the bathroom. As she sat on the toilet, feeling drunk and impulsive, she opened WhatsApp (WhatsApp is a messenger application on a phone, typically used to connect long distance) and texted Madison: *Wish you were here right now, I want you so bad.* Within minutes, Madison responded: *Same. Tell me how you want me to touch you.* Laura felt her heartbeat increasing. The conversation escalated from there, but I'll let you use your imagination.

ANALYSIS: WHAT IS SEXTING?

Earlier studies defined sexting as the sending of nude or partially nude photographs over text message. However, the definition has expanded to include

sexually explicit and suggestive words, as well. Think about your own definition of sexting. Where did you first learn about it? What are your associations
with the word?

Ever wonder where the term "sexting" came from? So did I, so I searched for
the origin of the word, eager to uncover its hidden roots. I was pleased to discover that in 2004, Canada's the *Globe and Mail* had an article about "explicit
text messages sent between David Beckham and an assistant that contained
what seems to be the first instance of the word's use in a newspaper."[1] The
article reported that "sext messaging" has a disinhibiting effect, like having
a couple of cocktails. Canada, the first country to invent that creative slang,
made me proud of my Canadian roots.

RL: U should see me, naked with only white cotton G-string. DB:
Love the sound of that cotton just *** *** getting more*** and your *** all
nice *** ***. And they say the age of romance is over.

Source: Josey Vogels, "Textual Gratification: Quill or Keypad, It's All about
Sex," *The Globe and Mail*, May 3, 2004, http://www.theglobeandmail.com/
technology/textual-gratification-quill-or-keypad-its-all-about-sex/article
1136823/. Used by permission of Josey Vogels.

The term "sext" went AWOL for a few years until the National Campaign
to Prevent Teen and Unplanned Pregnancy and Cosmogirl.com released a
survey in December 2008 that "detailed the popularity of explicit images or
texts being exchanged between teenagers without explicitly using the word
'sext.'"[2] The survey found "roughly 1 in 5 teens had been engaged in sending
naked pictures to one another."

The repercussions of sexting can be life altering as the picture or the text
sent is irrevocable. These images or words can easily be forwarded to others or posted on social media. Underage adolescents feel that taking pictures
of themselves naked may earn them popularity and attention, or they may
impulsively post without being mindful of the implications. They could then
find themselves in a legal situation when adults view these pictures and are
caught by the authorities. Unfortunately, role modeling this behavior are many
YouTube stars and famous personalities who reached stardom after exposing their bodies and leaking sex tapes. If you are interested in learning more
about this trend you can go to KidsHealth.org[3] or read articles written by
Mark Theoharis[4] about teen sexting laws. In a later chapter, I discuss how parents can specifically help their children avoid these predicaments as they enter
the world of relationships, sex, and technology.

Although sexting in itself has wide-ranging implications, the focus here will be its impact on dating and relationships. Both the consequences and benefits of sexting will be thoroughly explored, as it is essential to adequately understand both sides to make a responsible personal choice. I will reemphasize this point in the summary, but the goal is not to direct you in either direction, but rather to help you reflect on your personal values. This reflection will allow you to make an educated decision about your own behavior in regard to sexting.

ANALYSIS: SEXTING AND INFIDELITY

Dr. Kimberly Young, founder of the Center for Internet Addiction, defined a cyber-affair as a romantic and/or sexual relationship that is initiated via online contact and maintained predominantly through electronic conversations that occur through e-mail and in virtual communities.[5]

Infidelity is not a new concept and cannot be blamed on technology. Someone might begin an extramarital affair for a range of reasons. It might occur when married men or women act out their dissatisfaction, finding another partner to fulfill their unmet needs. They might initially develop an emotional connection, which may or may not turn physical. According to Shirley Glass, author of NOT "Just Friends": Protect Your Relationship from Infidelity and Heal the Trauma of Betrayal, an overwhelming majority of her clients did not seek out opportunity.[6] Their affairs began from being social acquaintances, neighbors, or workplace colleagues. Therefore, the outside relationship could have started platonic, then approached the slippery slope, and finally made its way across the line. According to Glass, "In many cases, the transition from friendship to affair is barely perceptible—to both participants and observers."[7] In these scenarios, technology was certainly not to blame for straying outside the marriage. An emotional connection happens naturally, when individuals are drawn to one another by an unexplainable force.

Sexting is a gradual and secretive way that people become increasingly intimate. Sometimes taken by surprise, the parties involved suddenly realize the level of their involvement has intensified beyond which they imagined when they initiated the process. According to a recent study that surveyed individuals from the site AshleyMadison.com, members use the Internet to find real-life partners, both for dating and for sex hookups.[8] Females are more likely than males to engage in sexting behaviors, while females and males are equally as likely to cheat both online and in real life while in serious real-life relationships. Approximately two-thirds of the women surveyed were more likely to send nude photographs or sexually explicit text messages compared to about half the men surveyed. Females in the 25–29 age group had the highest incidence of sexting.

For both men and women, however, the researchers noted that the best predictor for developing an extramarital relationship was engaging in cybersex, which often followed sexting. For women, engaging in cybersex tripled their odds of straying online and doubled their odds of cheating offline, while for men, having cybersex quintupled the odds of developing an online extramarital relationship and slightly less than doubled the odds for cheating offline. In general, exchanging sexually explicit chat and photos with another person online was a major indicator that the person in question was about to or planned to begin a physical relationship. In this respect, you can clearly see how technology plays a major role in escalating relationships.

In previous chapters, I mentioned how technology can instigate and promote jealousy. Although the apps provide an easy route to find a partner, sexting provides an acceptable buffer between flirtation and physicality. It enables people to test the waters and provides a fantasy image. At a certain juncture, this scheme may be fulfilled, although odds are they will not come to fruition exactly as imagined! On a side note, with the invention of virtual reality, the lines will become even more blurred between fantasy and reality.

Some couples consider sexting with an outside partner to be just as bad, if not worse, than physical infidelity. One reason is that their attention while home is directed to an outside party, even though their partner is potentially available. It also arguably develops a different level of intimacy than a one-night stand. The consistency and buildup of the texting tension is difficult for partners to absorb. Monica Whitty, interviewed individuals about their perceptions of online and offline infidelity.[9] Participants indicated that sexual acts online posed a greater threat than other acts such as viewing pornography. Whitty concluded that individuals are most concerned when their partner has desire for another and is seeking out a sexual encounter with an individual other than themselves. According to Whitty, "When considering sexual fantasies, the greater the threat of the sexual fantasy to the relationship, the more likely the fantasy is considered to be unfaithful."[10] This supports my own findings that an online affair can be perceived similarly to, or even more harmful than, a spontaneous physical encounter.

Some clients are unable to forgive their partners for sexting with another person. Others work in therapy with their partners to increase trust, intimacy, and emotional connection. Invariably, therapy involves commitment and acknowledgment of the need to change. Taking personal responsibility for one's hurtful action may be easier with a physical affair. Justifying sexting by "it was just over the phone" is sometimes a defensive excuse, which precludes recognizing the significance of the behavior to a partner. This could be a result of attachment, dependency, or in relation to the length of time and frequency of infidelity.

ANALYSIS: SEXTING ON THE CLOUD

Dr. Michael Salter led a focus group of young Australians aged 18–20 years old to examine how they negotiate privacy and publicity in their use of online and digital technology. Dr. Salter found that the widespread presence of girls and women on social media has sparked concern over their vulnerability to abuse or harm online.[11]

According to Salter, "The exchange of 'nudes' in the context of a consensual relationship was an intimate practice that could be desired by both parties. However, participants also described incidents in which it was not sexual desire but rather the pursuit of cultural capital among male peers that motivated boys to ask girls for 'nudes.'"[12] As described by participants, this sometimes occurred in a destructive manner as boys and men flattered girls and women in an attempt to gain images from them with the hidden intention of showing them to others later. When they received images and shared them with their peers, it was a way to increase popularity and social hierarchy.

Have you ever shared an attractive nude image that you found on the Internet with your friends? Once you send the image and receive feedback, how do you feel? Some men I've spoken to have indicated that it makes them feel more masculine. They claim it creates a bonding experience where they can fantasize together about the bodies they find attractive.

In the opposite respect, multiple female participants in this study described receiving unsolicited photos of male genitals (known colloquially as "dick pics") from male acquaintances and friends. This put them in an uncomfortable and difficult position. Overall, since they didn't know the motivations behind the images, they didn't know how to respond.

Some participants in the study spoke with sadness about the loss of friendships with boys and men who they felt could no longer be trusted because they had sent them "dick pics" or had circulated "nudes" of other girls and women. It was clear that both male and female participants valued their platonic opposite-sex friendships, and these could be put at risk by male perpetration of online abuse.

Ultimately, Salter found that whether girls and women were depicted in bodily images circulated without their consent, or they received unwanted images of male bodies, they became objects of attention and scrutiny in a manner that boys did not.

Many females I have spoken with have indicated they have received unwanted "dick pics" through the dating apps messaging systems. Some shake it off and delete the images, while others feel violated and disgusted. Some women find it humorous and use it as a good conversation starter. It is impossible to control what images you receive, which creates more questions about how to protect your privacy and boundaries.

Snapchat is an app that was initially used to send provocative images because the pictures are automatically deleted in a matter of seconds. However, a feature allows members to screenshot images. Even if Snapchat did not provide this feature, there were many ways that users could hack the app to save photos. This is just one example of the danger of assuming your pictures are private.

Another assumption is that the person you are dating would never cross you or hurt you by sending your pictures to their friends. I think it is safe to say that although your relationship might be "perfect" right now, we never know what the future holds. If one day something goes terribly wrong in your relationship, I don't think you want your partner holding onto a naked picture of you.

ANALYSIS: BENEFITS OF SEXTING

Now for the fun stuff. Sexting can be a helpful tool to enhance a relationship for numerous reasons. It gives you a chance to reveal your fantasies to your partner. It is also a way to let your partner know you are thinking about them physically throughout the day. In the next chapter, I will discuss how technology is beneficial in long-distance relationships. Sexting is a great way to keep up the physical connection while being miles away. Laura and Madison utilized sexting through WhatsApp to re-create the passion they experienced in Sydney. Receiving a text is exciting, especially when it is from a partner for whom you yearn intimately. It can be exhilarating to receive a sexual text from a partner that remains a secret between the two of you. Sexting provides continuity of sexual tension when physical distance is the reality in an intimate relationship.

INCREASING SEXUAL TENSION

Sexual tension is a social phenomenon that occurs when two individuals interact, either physically or remotely, and one or both feel a buildup of sexual desire, but physical touch is postponed.

Sexting can be invigorating, arousing, and a sexy secret between you and your partner. Throughout the day, you are consumed with work, stress, big ideas, and wandering thoughts. Perhaps the last thing on your mind is being intimate and physical with your partner later in the day, especially past the honeymoon stage.

However, sexting with your partner is quick, easy, can incite intimacy, and can lead to a better sexual experience later on. Texts such as "I can't wait to see you naked" or "I'm looking forward to touching you later" can ignite excitement and arousal. This can enhance your partner's day, remind them that you are thinking about them, and ultimately increase your sexual chemistry.

When you get home or meet up with your partner, you are already aroused. You want them even more because your imagination ran wild all day. The anticipation of what could happen is now within reach. You shared in a secret all day with your partner, sexting while your coworkers were sitting at their desks beside you. That surreptitious back and forth is hot and steamy. It's almost like you are both CIA agents, on a covert mission—aka Brad and Angelina in the movie *Mr. and Mrs. Smith*.

Then, when you see your partner, the agent mask flies off (or stays on if you want to role-play) and the action begins. That whole day, filled with giddy excitement, leads up to this very moment. Dopamine (a neurotransmitter that helps control the brain's reward and pleasure centers) builds while you wait, creating an even bigger sensation when receiving the reward.

Not everyone is a fan of sexting; however, the concept of sexting actually encompasses a range of erotic messages. The assumption is that sexting implies sending nude photos or speaking with extremely vulgar language. In actuality, sexting can be whatever you want it to be. One couple I work with sends emojis (small digital images or icons used to express an idea, emotion, etc., in electronic communication) to each other throughout the day. These emojis can insinuate a multitude of sexual innuendos left up to the imagination of each individual. The enjoyment for this couple is interpreting the emojis, letting their thoughts run wild. They end up laughing at each other's use of emojis, while simultaneously feeling aroused. For them, no nude pictures are sent and no words are texted. They found their own unique way to sext that brings additional pleasure to their relationship.

CASE STUDY: SEXTING FOR WHOM?

Ethan, a 36-year-old male, and Stephanie, a 35-year-old female, have been married for nine years. They have a four-year-old son and a one-year-old son. They came to therapy because their sex life started to diminish two years ago, and they were constantly arguing about it. Ethan felt completely neglected and expressed that Stephanie was directing all of her physical touch and energy toward the kids.

Stephanie felt exhausted from taking care of the kids and acknowledged a diminished sex drive. She claimed that the way Ethan initiated sex made her uncomfortable and that he attempted to be physical at the worst times. Ethan responded that there was never a good time and that she would reject him regardless.

During that first session, I asked Stephanie and Ethan to take the Love Language Questionnaire. This is a survey, based on a book by Gary Chapman, you can take to determine your specific "love language" in a relationship.[13] The potential answers are quality time, physical touch, words of affirmation, acts of service, and receiving gifts. Ethan scored the highest on physical touch, and Stephanie scored highest on quality time. Both Stephanie and Ethan wanted to improve their intimacy and sex life but were unsure how to get on the same page.

ANALYSIS: WHAT WENT WRONG?

After having children, parents struggle with allocating their time, as well as the emotional and physical connection between their partner and their children. The lack of intimacy between partners decreases, as does their desire to be physical with one another. Throughout life, there are peaks and valleys when it comes to sex drive. At certain points in life, especially when there are hormonal changes, the desire to be physical can heighten or diminish. After childbirth, it may be difficult to regain self-image as a sexy lover rather than "mother." Women's bodies change shape, which creates body image issues and which directly correlates with levels of desire. Stephanie cared deeply for Ethan and wanted to make him happy. She understood that in order for him to feel loved, he needed to receive physical touch. She was not sure how to increase her drive and how to feel the desire she once had. Ethan also understood how difficult it was to care for two young children and appreciated all the work that Stephanie did throughout the day. However, he couldn't help feeling constantly rejected, neglected, and unloved. Sex and intimacy was an essential need for him, and he was tired of begging and fighting for her attention.

THERAPY: ACCEPTING THE "OTHER"

Stephanie and Ethan both wanted to feel intimate with each other, but what did that really mean to each of them? For Ethan, having intercourse was his way of feeling close to and accepted by Stephanie. He understood that their lives were completely overwhelmed with responsibilities; however, he could not grasp why intercourse was not a priority in their relationship. He was willing to make compromises in his day to make time for intimacy and felt that Stephanie was not willing to do the same. Stephanie also valued physical touch and, more importantly, cared deeply about Ethan's happiness. She was aware that she was experiencing a reduction in their emotional connection and related this to less quality time. She also knew that this dramatically affected her level of sexual arousal. However, she couldn't fathom how to make a shift in their relationship with the reality of their busy lifestyles.

THERAPY: HOW SEXTING CAN HELP

Sexting was one strategy implemented with Stephanie and Ethan to improve their physical and sexual connection. Sexting can be useful for all couples, regardless of the longevity of their relationship. It is a way for couples to re-create and redefine their sexual chemistry when there is a limited amount of private time in the household. Telling a partner "I can't wait to kiss you later" takes a couple of seconds out of your day, and can lead to big rewards. Prior to this intervention, both Stephanie and Ethan shared the content of their previous text conversations. Limited to navigating childrearing responsibilities and daily chores, there was little opportunity for the expression of passion, desire, or lust. This represents a majority of conversations parents engage in post-childbirth.

Sexting enabled Stephanie and Ethan to rekindle a heightened awareness of their attraction to one another despite the tumult often associated with balancing work and kids. Depending on the message, it either increased sexual tension or provided emotional support, creating a much-needed intimate connection. Stephanie would also feel aroused during these messages. It was a bit outside her comfort zone and a nice change of pace from changing diapers and breastfeeding. She felt sexy again from the words in his text. It also gave her a chance to express her sexual fantasies to Ethan in a way that felt comfortable to her. Although the sexting did not always lead to physical touch, Ethan felt more assured in the relationship. Sexting was a technique we used throughout the course of therapy. It was a unique way to utilize technology to aid in increasing intimacy, sexual chemistry, and sexual tension. Small changes in a relationship can yield big rewards.

Quality time was also a necessary component in increasing intimacy for Stephanie. Sexting aided in increasing their desire to make concrete private plans for themselves later in the evening. As they texted each other throughout the day, they would make statements like "I'll meet you in the basement at 8" or "Don't come into the bedroom until 9:15." Ethan would sometimes surprise Stephanie by drawing her a bath or setting a romantic scene. Regardless of the evening activity, Stephanie was pleased that they were spending real time together and Ethan was excited that they were becoming more physical.

SEXTING EXPECTATIONS VERSUS REALITY

Perceived expectations as to how a sexting conversation will unfold can easily be miscommunicated. The best parallel example for explaining this to couples is to compare it to porn. When your idea of sex is "porn sex," you generally are displeased when your partner does not moan, when the penis is not erect for hours, or when the penis does not slide in easily. In other words, people get courageous when sexting. In sexting, you can bend yourself in all sorts of ways, use discourse that you don't even know how to pronounce, and have intercourse in the wildest of places.

When you finally see your partner at the end of the day, week, or month (for those long-distancers), the experience can look quite different. If you set proper expectations, then you will not be as disillusioned. Perhaps you can attempt the positions that you described in vast detail, but be careful to avoid injury! It also can be a way to gain a better understanding of your partner's fantasy. If you find your partner constantly mentioning a squeeze, slap, touch, or grab of the glutes, it might be a good idea to try butt play.

Some individuals express in therapy how they expected to be aggressively handled as soon as they walked in the door, due to the sexting conversation they had earlier with their partner. They felt discontented, hurt, and confused when the night ended with a lack of intercourse or with "vanilla" intercourse (sex that involves no kinkiness or BDSM of any kind). Couples should work on communicating about fantasy play and explicitly request certain positions, actions, and behaviors. Although it might be easier to initially assert yourself through sexting, your partner might not interpret your sentiment as a genuine desire.

In the book *Frequently Asked Questions about Texting, Sexting, and Flaming*, author Rebecca Klein stated, "If you decide to sext with someone, it is important to be clear about your intentions and to know what the other person's intentions are. You need to be clear about whether what you are saying is hypothetical or if you intend to follow through on any of it. This can help lessen the risk of awkward or dangerous situations occurring in person."[14]

Communicating clearly is the key to a healthy sex and sext life. Clarify your desires, describe your fantasies, and set your boundaries. From there, the sexual relationship will grow naturally.

IMPLICATIONS FOR THERAPISTS

Psychoeducation

First, explore your client's definition of sexting and their motivation behind the behavior. Part of treatment might include informing or educating about potential consequences. Younger clients who screenshot sexting conversations and distribute them to their friends may assume the information will be kept private. Their immaturity precludes their understanding of potential implications. Understanding the reason your client is deciding to sext would be helpful in navigating this therapeutic process. Here are some sample questions to ask your client:

1. Are you engaging in sexting to appeal to a partner?
2. Are you in a long-term relationship with your partner?
3. Do you feel safe with and trusting of your partner?
4. Are you sending sexts to increase sexual chemistry?
5. Are you sending sexts to inform your partner of your sexual preferences?

Much like an intake, these questions will help a therapist meet the client where he or she is to develop an appropriate strategy. If the client is engaging in risky, harmful behavior, psychoeducation would be a suitable first step. Additionally, therapists should be aware of the laws in relation to teen sexting in their state, specifically pertaining to their mandatory reporting obligations. When sexting is not counterproductive to personal goals nor ego dystonic, it can be helpful to show support while normalizing the behavior.

MOTIVATIONAL INTERVIEWING

A person who is utilizing sexting needs to be cognizant as to why, when, and to whom they are using this form of communication. Self-awareness will enable the individual to feel comfortable with her choices and to create safe boundaries. This is the best protection from getting herself into an irrevocable situation.

Motivational interviewing is a powerful technique that uses open-ended questions, reflective listening, empathy, inspiring statements, and reframing. These principles of motivational interviewing can be useful to help your client increase awareness and be in control of his sexting behavior. First, understand if he experiences sexting as an issue. If he feels troubled by this behavior, is it because he is acting outside of his comfort zone, but not harming anyone including himself, and does he have an overly vigilant superego? On the other hand, is she putting herself and/or others at risk and so is coming for help to control it? Regardless, these techniques will guide the session so that the client will be mindful of behavior, thoughts, and feelings.

Open-ended questions: This type of question encourages people to respond with more a simple "yes" or "no" answer. Try to incorporate the client's own language within the question by mirroring back previous sentiments. If a client uses the terminology "sexting" or "sext," then these are examples of good open-ended questions. If he just describes the behavior without labeling, it is helpful you to do the same.

Examples:

- Tell me about your initial perceptions of sexting.
- Explain your thought process prior to sending out a sext.
- Prior to sexting, did you participate in other actions that enabled you to share your body openly?
- How would you describe your body expression in your most recent sext?

You can see that clients would have to respond to these questions with a thoughtful answer. They enable the client to share her perceptions of herself in reference to her behavior. This begins the therapeutic process of meeting the client where he is and encourages him to self-reflect.

Reflective listening: In order to confirm that a client feels unmistakably understood, a therapist will repeat back what he or she heard. Additionally, therapists might infer other ideas from the client's statement and want to ensure that they are accurate. Sometimes, to check out validity it helps to end the question with "is that correct?" or "am I getting there?"

Examples:

- It sounds like you initially thought sexting was a funny, inconsequential activity.
- So it seems you changed your perception after starting to sext with your last partner.
- [Combining reflective listening and open ended questioning] You seem to be describing some type of rush after sexting? Can you talk about that some more?

After practicing reflective listening, the client either will agree and continue to expand their thought, or she will correct your misinterpretation by clarifying or rephrasing her previous statement.

Inspiring, motivating statements: For this step, I find myself building on the client's strengths by offering encouragement and acknowledging positive steps. It is helpful for a client to recognize the favorable aspects of his or her life. This creates optimism for him or her when tackling difficult topics and issues. Follow-up questions give clients a chance to voice their own personal growth for themselves. They also tend to be more optimistic and open to creating additional goals once they hear their strengths voiced aloud.

Examples:

- You are great at articulating your thought processes and feelings. Is that something you've noticed?
- You clearly demonstrate an extensive understanding for why you engage in sexting. It is impressive! When have you processed this and what has that been like for you?
- You appear to be very open minded, understanding, and supportive of your partner. I am wondering if that plays a role in your decision to sext.

Empathy: Therapists utilize active listening to understand the vulnerabilities and feelings of a client. Many clients are sharing difficult narratives for the first time or have been shut down in the past when attempting to disclose. Therefore, showing support and empathy is imperative when building rapport with a client. Sexting is a sensitive, personal topic that could be difficult and embarrassing to expose. Therapists should refrain from showing judgment or biases to avoid shaming the client.

Examples:

- Wow, it sounds like that was a very vulnerable time period for you. Opening up in that way toward your partner can be a very emotional experience.
- Your willingness to acknowledge areas where you need to grow is impressive.

- Your desire to share on an intimate level is understandably frustrating when you feel that your partner is not at the same place. I can understand how lonely that experience must be for you at times.

At this point, you have developed a close relationship with your client. Providing empathy and feedback allows you to take a more active role, while still keeping the focus on your client. Some patients have difficulty accepting empathy and sometimes will experience their therapist as being condescending. The skill in transmitting empathy lies in the ability to correctly evaluate your client's feelings and respond to them without excessive patronization.

Summarize and/or develop discrepancy: The previous steps will illuminate the client's feelings and motivations behind the sexting behavior. If it is determined that the client feels confident and secure with the behavior, you can summarize and transition to the next topic.

Examples:

- After delving into your previous and current attitudes toward sexting, it sounds like you really care about your partner and that sexting only enhances the connection and intimacy. Does that sound right?

- It sounds like you are not entirely confident in your decision to start sexting with your boyfriend. You mentioned that you feel pressure to sext in order to keep the passion alive. I am wondering if you feel comfortable discussing this with him?

- You seem to be really happy with your partner and want to pursue sexting to build chemistry. You wanted to discuss the possible consequences and we went over some of your concerns. How do you feel about sexting moving forward?

If it is determined that the behavior is ego dystonic (does not match up with his or her values or superego), you can begin to develop discrepancy. Exploring the consequences of the behavior helps clients examine the driving force. Are the consequences worth the action? Or are they not feeling good about it because they are not getting the response they are seeking from their sexting? Or are they feeling shamed by their friends who are judging them?

Examples:

- Tell me what concerns you about sexting and what motivates you to sext?
- What will happen if you continue to sext? What are some possible outcomes?
- How would you feel if you never began to sext or if you stopped sexting now?

The client may start to recognize ambivalence toward sexting. Part of the exploration requires discussing how sexting relates to other treatment issues. Throughout these inquiries, the therapist needs to come back to the question of whether the behavior is ultimately in conflict with the client's overall goals. If so, seek to determine the needs that sexting is fulfilling and possible replacement behaviors that may be just as, if not more, rewarding.

ENHANCING COMMUNICATION

Sexting can be beneficial in increasing intimacy, in building sexual chemistry, and in helping couples connect when long distance. However, issues might arise when fantasy does not convert to reality. Therefore, couples should work on exploring how sexting will be used in their relationship during a session. Turning toward one another, couples will discuss the type of sexting they want to engage in, and how they envision it playing out in person. Some couples might create boundaries and determine that they only want to sext in the morning because they have busy meetings in the afternoon and need to con-centrate. Partners might also decide certain language that is acceptable to use in their sexts. It is a myth that sexting must include vulgar language. I explain to clients that sexting can consist of a wide range of terminology and level of vulgarity. Additionally, some clients assume that sexting indicates a desire to "dirty talk" in the bedroom. However, many of my clients specifically opt to sext due to the inhibition they experience during sexual intercourse. It is difficult for them to state their preferences, and they find it easier to commu-nicate through this process. If this is the case, I found it helpful to encourage my clients to sext consistently and then they became increasingly comfortable with orally disclosing their desires.

SUMMARY

At the end of the day, you make your own decisions and control your own body. You have a right to decide who has the privilege of seeing images of yourself. My advice is to hold off until you feel committed, safe, and secure with your partner. Sexting can be a positive addition to your repertoire; however, it can also affect future relationships, have a negative impact on an already-difficult breakup, and can become evidence for an affair. So use judgment and educate yourself about saving and sending images.

Sometimes the ease of posting and texting can make us forget about the potential implications of our actions. We cannot immediately see the reper-cussions or consequences. Additionally, we act impulsively in the heat of the moment, when we want an immediate reward. It is easy to quickly snap a picture or send a sext, as our phones are with us at all times. More accessible tools require more purposeful behavior.

Try to be mindful about why you are engaging in sexting behavior. What are you trying to communicate to your partner? Is it enjoyable because you are building additional sexual tension? Are you apprehensive about verbally expressing your preferences for fear of rejection? Are you sending sexts to appeal to your partner because that is their preference in terms of arousal? Before deciding if this is a behavior you want to change, it is beneficial to ask yourself these questions.

If you are a therapist working with teens who are sexting, it is important to educate them about the potential outcomes without appearing judgmental. This can be challenging when young adults feel confident about their decision and are enjoying the sexting experience. During the teenage years, risk-taking behaviors are more prevalent and weighing future implications is of little concern. The conversation regarding sexting could be included with a general conversation about control over one's own body and self-respect. Lesson plans that revolve around healthy relationships could also include conversations about appropriate texting and calling behaviors.

P.S.: Be careful when drinking and sexting. . . . For obvious reasons.

Chapter 8

THE NEW LONG DISTANCE

CASE STUDY: HARRY AND BETH'S LONG-DISTANCE LOVE

Harry and Beth are both 29 years old. They met two years ago at a networking event for foodies in Boston. They both enjoyed attending these events for the free food and alcohol, and to meet other "food-crazed junkies." Harry owned numerous grilled cheese food trucks, and Beth worked in catering. They highlighted their initial encounter during the first therapy appointment.

Harry: "When I saw Beth at the networking event, I was immediately attracted to her spunky style and positive aura. She was wearing this colorful dress and high boots. Super sexy. I watched her sneak to the food and alcohol table in between every conversation and found it hilarious and endearing."

Beth: "Wow. I can't believe he remembers that [laughs]. All I remember is this nerdy-looking guy in glasses coming up to me by the alcohol table and saying, 'So are you also primarily here for the free stuff?' I remember chatting after that for the rest of the event and then post-gaming at one of his grilled cheese trucks. His grilled cheeses are by far the best in Boston, so that immediately won my heart. I guess the rest is history."

Harry and Beth's relationship was exciting. They traveled to different countries, exploring the unique cultures and cuisines. They even started a travel blog together, building a website and uploading their photos of the amazing dishes they tried. Toward the end of the second year of their courtship, Beth began to tire of the catering world. Throughout her life, Beth enjoyed cooking. She found the experience relaxing and cathartic. After traveling with Harry, she also discovered her passion for ethnic food. One morning, Beth woke up and a light-bulb went off. She realized she desperately wanted to be a chef and imagined opening up her own distinctive restaurant with a food theme of East meets West. She spent that entire day researching culinary institutes and found one that truly sparked her interest. Unfortunately, it was located in Belize. Although Harry's schedule was flexible, he needed to live primarily in Boston. Beth was nervous, scared, and exhilarated all at the same time. Later that night, over dinner, she anxiously shared with Harry her revelation and the predicament it caused.

ANALYSIS: HARRY AND BETH'S RELATIONSHIP

Although Harry and Beth were still in the exploration phase of their relation-ship, they felt confident that they wanted to be together and work through any hardships that stepped foot in their path. Harry was an entrepreneur and understood the ideology of following Beth's passion, regardless of where it takes you. He cared about Beth tremendously, wanted her to be happy, and therefore supported her decision to apply to the culinary school in Belize.

Once Beth was accepted to the program, they came to therapy to discuss ways to continue and further enhance their relationship from across seas. Beth felt confident in her feelings for Harry and did not want her professional dream to interfere with or hurt the emotional connection they shared. Both Beth and Harry felt strongly about creating a concrete plan, exploring different products, and attempting different techniques to make the relationship work.

THERAPY: THE PRE-DISTANCE WORKUP

The first tools we discussed were the basic Facetime (Internet-based video calling app on Apple phones) and texting protocols. We looked into the time difference and discovered that Boston is two hours ahead of Belize. This alleviated some of their anxiety, as they both assumed it would be a much greater time difference. They both agreed that talking on the phone in the morning would be helpful in starting the day off right. Harry would text Beth when he woke up, and when Beth was getting ready for class she would call Harry to check in. They both appreciated casual check-ins throughout the day. Beth was unsure of her schedule but agreed to enlighten Harry as soon as she received the day-to-day class times. They both agreed to download WhatsApp, or their phone bills would soar.

Physical intimacy was a huge part of their relationship. Aside from inter-course, they both felt strongly about touch as a means to express affection and love. They acknowledged that the distance would affect their ability to be physical and were open to exploring any products that would help.

Some of the products I highlight in this chapter were used by Harry and Beth, while others are toys that came to market after they ended treatment. Both Harry and Beth found sexting (described in the previous chapter) a necessary complement to using these products. Sexting provided them with the ability to express their desire for each other while Beth was in class. Even though the result might have ended with self-masturbation with or without a sex toy, the buildup of sexual tension was a nice element of "foreplay." It was also helpful due to their difference in time zone, as Harry sometimes went to bed before Beth could chat on the phone.

ANALYSIS: PRODUCTS FOR LONG-DISTANCE RELATIONSHIPS (LDRs)

OhMiBod: I spoke to OhMiBod founder Brian Dunham about his products. When discussing the theme of sex and tech, he stated, "The idea is to take technology and make it easy to use and fun to play with" (Brian Dunham, personal communication). His products are vibrators that connect to an app and are controlled via Bluetooth and WiFi. His wireless music vibrator takes "whatever music you feel sexy with and takes the base and rhythm and translates that through pulse with modulation to actual vibrations." Over video chat, Harry would play a song that he knew would arouse Beth (he knew he could always get her with a Ja-Rule beat). The beat of the music would translate into the vibrations of the toy. Harry could also control the vibrations by using the app on his phone. They had fun while connecting in an intimate way.

Lovense: Harry and Beth loved the vibrator produced by Lovense. They took the traditional rabbit vibrator and made it easy to operate from long distance, also using Bluetooth wireless. Through the app on the phone, Harry and Beth were able to video chat, message each other, and Harry was able to control the vibrations. Beth also loved the rabbit vibrator to use on her own when Harry wasn't available. Harry enjoyed the experience because there was also a toy for him to use simultaneously. When he slid the masturbator onto his penis, the head of Beth's sex toy began rotating. The faster he moved the toy up and down, the faster her vibrator moved. He also expressed that his toy simulated the sensation he felt when he was physically inside her.

Vibease: Beth loved Vibease, but not primarily for the long-distance component. She enjoyed how the vibrator synced with erotic audio. She would listen to erotic stories and use the vibrator. Although she enjoyed these moments without Harry, she would communicate with him and describe the experience later in the day. Harry loved hearing Beth discuss the pleasure she felt from the stories. The image replayed in his mind as he masturbated.

THERAPY: OPEN COMMUNICATION

Although Beth and Harry were open-minded and willing to explore different techniques and products, they realized soon after moving apart that they would have to adapt and learn skills to communicate more effectively from long distance. They were both used to having daily shared experiences, which enabled the relationship to progress. Communication in regard to physical intimacy was natural, as they were able to read each other's nonverbal cues and would make adaptations based on the other's body language.

Beth and Harry had to be creative in terms of designing shared experiences. They watched *Game of Thrones* and *The Bachelor* religiously. Therefore, the nights those shows aired, they facetimed while watching and would laugh and discuss during the commercials. Harry and Beth recorded the episode with DVR so that they could watch it together despite the time difference. Although they missed the physical touch component, they refused to give up this aspect of their relationship. They enjoyed casually glancing at the other's facial expression during the episodes. This consistency helped them feel a sense of normalcy in their relationship.

Communicating about the sexual nature of their relationship proved to be more challenging. Foreplay and the initiating dialogue looked completely different. Due to the distance, they lost the spontaneity component. Harry and Beth had to plan and discuss over text or phone when they wanted to utilize the vibrators. They had to verbally indicate their level of arousal. They were still able to demonstrate pleasure with nonverbal cues; however, they had to learn to focus on the camera while enjoying their own touch.

When they first began their LDR, the conversations were awkward and felt unnatural. Harry would say things like, "So . . . wanna give it a shot?" or Beth would text him during class and say, "Vibrator tonight?" Neither of those questions is uncomfortable or strange in any way; however, they did not do the trick of arousing either partner. After a couple weeks of failed attempts at initiating long-distance sex, they scheduled a Skype session with me to discuss ways to change their communication style.

One of the themes of the session was language. What language aroused each partner? How did Harry want Beth to inform him that she wanted to use the vibrator? How did Beth want Harry to voice his fantasy through text? We discussed different scenarios and mapped out possible sexts. For example, during the day when Beth was in class, she welcomed the text, "Excited for our alone time later," or at night, when Harry was hanging out in his apartment, he appreciated the text, "On my way home, thinking about your touch." By the end of the session both Beth and Harry had a better idea of the type of language that would spark the other's desire.

RESEARCH: INTIMACY IN LDR (LONG-DISTANCE RELATIONSHIP) VERSUS GC (GEOGRAPHICALLY CLOSE)

L. Crystal Jiang and Jeffrey T. Hancock studied levels of intimacy as a direct result of adaptive behaviors in LDRs.[1] They recruited 67 heterosexual dating couples from several communication and psychology classes.

Some research suggests that long-distance romantic relationships enjoy as much or even more trust and satisfaction than geographically close relationships.[2] Jiang and Hancock wanted to test an intimacy-enhancing process, in which long-distance couples engaged in more self-disclosure and perceived partner responsiveness. According to Jiang and Hancock, this process results in a greater level of intimacy. They define self-disclosure as the "communication of personal facts, thoughts, and emotions to another."[3] Perceived partner responsiveness "is the perception that the relationship partner recognizes, values, and behaviorally supports the core aspects of the self."[4]

They described the development of intimacy in the following manner: "Intimacy develops when one party (termed the discloser) reveals personally relevant information, thoughts, or feelings to the partner (the disclosive act). It continues when the partner's response addresses the specific content of the disclosure and conveys understanding, validation, and caring for the discloser (the responsive act)."[5]

The results found that long-distance daters increased self-disclosures and idealized their partner's disclosures, leading ultimately to more intimacy. According to Jiang and Hancock, self-disclosure leads to perceived partner responsiveness, which in turn increases intimacy. This process was found to be stronger for LDR than for GC couples. This suggests that, relative to GC daters, the intimacy that LDR daters experience is more dependent on the perceptions of being understood, validated, and cared for by their partners.

These findings align with previous research that shows when interactions move from face-to-face (fTf) to a text-based, asynchronous (not occurring in real time) environment, people adapt and change their behaviors to meet their interpersonal needs. Two of the changes include selective self-presentation and uncertainty-reducing strategies. In other words, partners are using other forms of communication more regularly to continue building the relationship from a distance. Examples include texting or calling while using public transportation or waiting in line at the supermarket. Successful LDRs entail couples using technology creatively to maintain communication that includes continuation of intimacy and sharing of vulnerabilities. Both partners need to be committed to each other and to making these changes in order to facilitate growth in the relationship.

So what does this research really mean for the modern-day LDR? Individuals in LDRs clearly have to adjust their behavior and communication style as seen in the relationship of Harry and Beth. However, there is a great deal of hope for these couples. As long as each partner is self-aware and cognizant of the adaptive behaviors, they can continue to develop emotional closeness from abroad. With the use of technology, such as Facetime or other video calls, text, e-mail, phone calls, and in some cases teledildonics (those long-distance vibrators), couples can improve communication styles and build intimacy.

The study also suggests that certain personality types would work better with LDRs. An openness to modify communication style, while co-creating new language and behavior, is a requirement for a successful LDR. Therefore, those individuals with personalities that are inflexible, stubborn, and fixed would find it more difficult to endure LDR. Just like any relationship, maintaining an emotional connection takes work and energy. However, enhancing a relationship without face-to-face interactions and shared in-person experiences entails an extra boost of strength, openness, and commitment.

RESEARCH: WILL MY LDR MAKE IT?

Marianne Dainton and Brooks Aylor, researchers at La Salle University, studied associations between communication channel use and relational maintenance by individuals in long-distance, romantic relationships. They collected survey data from 114 individuals in LDRs.[6]

Dainton and Aylor began with the understanding that LDRs often involve uncertainty about the nature of the relationship. They include in their analysis the hypothesis that individuals who are insecure about their relationship might seek reassurance through oral channels. That is, they may need to talk to or see their relational partner for reassurance. Therefore, if they are looking for immediacy, which may be integral to effectively communicating reassurance, written channels such as e-mail and texting are not useful. On the other hand, those who need to see their partner might also find it difficult and costly to do so. Long-distance phone conversations, after all, are often costly. It is possible the financial situations of these partners dictate they make more use of written and computer-mediated channels, which are relatively inexpensive and convenient methods of communication.

The researchers concluded that communication style (written versus oral) is also a personal preference. This parallels what I find in the couples I work with. The researchers found that telephone use was significantly related to the performance of three maintenance behaviors: assurances, openness, and shared tasks. Reassurances may be perceived as more genuine, and thus be more effective, if presented orally or in face-to-face situations. Each LDR is unique and requires open and honesty in regard to communication preference.

So, how is this research useful for *you*? Well, there is no specific time length implied in the definition of long-distance romantic relationship. Therefore, this research can provide useful conversation starters even if you or partner travels for a week for work. Prior to separating, you and partner can discuss your preferred channels to communicate affection, assurance, and simple updates.

In the case of Harry and Beth, they communicated through text about their day, classes, and basic frustrations. In the morning and at night, they spoke on the phone or with a video call. During this time, they usually provided validation or assurance through words of affirmation. They expressed how much they missed one another, loved each other, and would discuss plans to see each other. Their long-distance experience was not flawless, but due to their preparation in discussing communication preferences, they had less anxiety about the relationship, less miscommunication, and fewer disagreements. The fact that this was time-limited was also a factor. Beth spent all of her semester breaks with Harry, and he took one two-week vacation per year to be with her. The potential success of this relationship was high because each of them sacrificed and persevered. It is likely that this long-distance phase will be looked back upon as a challenge they creatively overcame and enjoyed.

RESEARCH: SOCIAL MEDIA AND LDRs

Another study conducted in 2013 by researchers at Chapman University analyzed the influence social media has on a romantic partner's satisfaction in an LDR.[7] One of the major findings was that 25 percent of partners in LDRs felt that social media caused miscommunications. This was a dominant reason as to why social media hurt geographically distant relationships. One participant stated, "There are things that don't translate through social media."[8] The researchers stated that misinterpretations and miscommunications are a common struggle in face-to-face communication and that they increase only when communicating through social media.

Due to the lack of nonverbal communication, 21 percent of participants felt they couldn't clearly convey messages, thoughts, and feelings to each other. Some participants stated, "I can't always read his expression, body language, tone or feelings," and "We can't use body language to communicate so our verbal communication needs to be much more clear."

Some participants (11%) felt that using social media simply intensified their feelings of missing their significant others more than if they did not use social media. However, other participants discussed how social media made them feel as though they were involved in the everyday lives of their significant other, whether that was because they were constantly texting throughout the day or seeing posted pictures on Facebook.

Overall, social media can clearly be either detrimental or useful in LDRs. The key is to communicate with each other about how you plan to use social media and if you are offended, hurt, or jealous by any post. Generally, if you are open and honest about your feelings toward one another and can verbalize those feelings using words of affirmation, then social media should not play a harmful role in the relationship.

THE FUTURE OF SEX, TECH, AND LONG-DISTANCE RELATIONSHIPS

The industry of sex and tech is just starting to boom. Bryony Cole, founder of the futureofsex podcast, explores how fast our society is evolving from sex clubs and teledildonics to sexual fluidity and erotic intelligence. She states that "technology has transformed the way we relate to each other. It's also changed the way we fall in love and even the way we have sex. Our digital and offline lives have become so intermingled that everything we do, including each other, has been affected."[9]

It is not surprising that people are hopping on the bandwagon of sex and tech, hoping to enhance LDRs. After all, statistics published in the *Journal of Communication* claim that three million married couples in the United States live apart and that 25–50 percent of college students are in LDRs.[10] Additionally, the remote work industry is growing tremendously. According to Global Workplace Analytics, regular work-at-home employment, among the non-self-employed population, has grown by 103 percent since 2005.[11] Additionally 3.7 million employees (2.8% of the workforce) now work from home at least half the time. This means that individuals are also able to travel, not take time off, and still complete their assignments.

INTERVIEW WITH CARMAN—TELEPRESENCE

As remote work and LDRs become more mainstream, the tech industry is advancing to keep up. Carman Neustadter (personal communication), founder of the Connections Lab, said he "found it personally challenging to stay connected with friends and family who lived far away."[12] He wanted to develop technology that would help people share their lives, regardless of distance. The Connections Lab, part of the School of Interactive Arts and Technology at Simon Frasier University in British Columbia, Canada, is researching and developing technology that connects us.

I spoke with Carman about a few of his studies and what he sees for the future of tech and LDRs. He began his work by looking at different types of relationships and how individuals connect either through video chat or Facetime. He conducted a study in 2012 in which he noticed that partners were leaving their webcams on while doing an activity during the day. It was as if they were virtually living together, while doing everyday ventures such as watching television, cooking in the kitchen, or doing laundry. Therefore, Carman and his team invented the telepresence robot. This robot wheels around your home with your partner's live video streaming from its face. Your partner can use an Xbox to control the movement of the robot. The robot can move around freely and look around the room. This invention completely changes how you are present with your partner from a remote location.

Carman noticed that the robot created more real-life experiences that are typically shared between partners. For example, he noticed that arguments, specifically, looked very different from a typical LDR. When couples disagreed, the partner controlling the robot can literally walk away from the conversation (instead of the classic hanging up). You can see and feel your partner's hurt, anger, and frustration by the movement. It completely changes the sense of control and power dynamics that are often present in long-term relationships.

The flex-and-feel gloves engineered by the lab were meant to simulate the feeling of touch. For example, partners were able to detect the bends in their fingers. This sent vibration patterns to their partner's glove. It acted like a ripple effect down the hand, and you could change the intensity of the vibration. The problem the lab faced was that people were just not ready to have only the simulation. They wanted to concurrently see their partner. Therefore, participants in the study used the combination of video chat with the gloves to create a complete in-person simulation.

Carman told me about other tech products for enhancing LDRs. Another lab is creating a vest that simulates the feeling of being hugged. It expands while you wear it so you feel the pressure and warmth of your partner. Another company has also created a hand-holding product where you can feel the warmth of your partner's hand.

Overall, Carman feels that moderation is needed. If there is over-usage, then we are simply too connected. He explained another study in which he tested out this phenomenon of being always connected to your partner. He studied two couples for a month. Each partner would keep his or her smartphone in his or her pocket sticking out for an entire day and would program the phone to be on Skype "autoanswer." This way partners could call each other at any time and see where they are. They also wore an earpiece so that when a partner started to speak, they would be able to respond automatically.

They found dramatically different results between each couple. One couple loved being able to check in with each other at any time. They were used to living together and were a more spontaneous couple, willing to try anything and everything. The female partner was especially open-minded and eager to try new products and devices to improve the relationship.

The second couple hated the constant access. They enjoyed and valued their nightly Skype sessions and felt that being constantly connected ruined their evening conversation. The female in the relationship was also controlling and hated interruptions. Overall, Carman agreed with my observation that certain couples are more equipped to thrive in LDRs with the assistance of tech products, based on their personalities as individuals and as a couple.

When discussing the future, Carman stated that he believes high-resolution video products will evolve faster and be distributed sooner. For example,

Facetime and Skype will be available in much better quality. He feels that products related to touch will take longer to hit the market because they are more taboo. Wearables are too new of an idea so it will take time to develop and become mainstream. Additionally, creating a touch product that creates an identical simulation to an in-person experience is difficult from an engineering perspective.

Humans are neither used to nor desire sacrificing live physical touch. They are, however, familiar with replacing face-to-face interactions with video calls. Carman informed me that in 1964, AT&T produced the first "picture phone" and introduced it at the New York World's Fair. However, it had to pull the plug in 1968, because customers just weren't interested. Carman explains that society needs to be ready for big change and sometimes it takes longer than we expect.

When I asked Carman what's next for him and his team, he expressed interest in exploring ways that people can create more shared leisured experiences from long distance, specifically outside the home. For example, his team is experimenting with ways for long-distance couples to share bike rides, sporting events, and hiking. Typically, in order for long-distance couples to connect, they have to be sitting in the home. He wants to change that mindset and encourage couples to venture outside, explore, and exercise, while still maintaining a connection from afar.

ANALYSIS: VIRTUAL REALITY (VR)

In the near future, dating via virtual reality will become as normal as online dating is now. It isn't a difficult conclusion to jump to as the industry is already creating apps specifically designed for socializing and meeting strangers. Individuals are excited by the prospect of appearing more confident and outgoing than their real selves. It is another way to mask their own insecurities, or perhaps a shy personality, and portray themselves as their ideal self-image.

This technology will transform how partners in LDRs connect. Eventually, it will be easier to overcome physical distance while maintaining a sense of connection. Again, there are multiple factors that affect the potential of LDRs being successful. The individuals both need to be open-minded and committed. The period of distance needs to be time-limited or have significant periods of scheduled physical closeness. The couple's relationship needs to be one worth preserving, meaning both partners are getting their needs met and have the capacity to expand their repertoire as to how to give to the other.

As this technology continues to develop, another question surfaces: How will this affect the desire to venture outside and interact face-to-face? If you can feel the touch of another, communicate, and create shared experiences without stepping outside your door, what will motivate you to ever leave?

Additionally, it will not be surprising if dating apps also utilize VR to build the setting of having a virtual date. How does this influence how individuals develop socially?

The evolution of VR presents clear benefits for improving long-distance friendships and romantic relationships. However, just like with anything, moderation is key. Balancing a VR relationship with in-person interactions is key in building a healthy lifestyle.

In order to better understand the world of VR and the impact it can have on LDRs, I spoke with Jason, 27, who utilized this technology with his ex-girlfriend (personal communication). He used a system called Vive, which he explained consisted of a headset, two "cube things" that you place on either side of the room, and controllers. He played in a small area of his apartment.

They decided to try out Vive when his girlfriend took an internship in the UK, while he stayed behind in California. She was away for a few months, and they were used to spending a significant amount of time together. He stated they also used Facetime and video chat, but VR was theoretically more imme-diate and felt more like being physically together.

They first created their avatars. Jason did not spend a ton of time creating his, as there was not much to work with besides hair color and basic effects. He stated that he grabbed the most basic-looking male. His girlfriend chose a ball-shaped robot, which, at a certain point, became "jarring, upsetting, even. She wasn't herself anymore. Or at least, not her VR self. My brain didn't like it one bit." He explained how he would hear her voice and see her mannerisms, but it just wasn't her, which is an odd feeling. The way you hold the controllers affects the movement in the game, but his brain also filled in the gaps where the simulation lacked. His girlfriend's nonverbal language was key for him to perceive her presence.

I inquired about how it affected their communication, in general. He stated that they definitely talked about it a lot throughout the day but that it was similar to speaking to your partner after seeing a movie. Because it is a shared experience, it becomes a topic of conversation. Although embarking on this journey started as a way to simulate the "date experience," his girlfriend began entering the game on her own, engaging with the mutual "friends" they made. It was a way for her to be social in a city she was unfamiliar with and alone. At first, he was confused and would say things like, "Why didn't you tell me you were playing," but after a while, he became more comfortable. His initial disappointment was a result of his expectation that they would use the game to hang out one-on-one. However, he had to admit that it was more exciting to hang together at the tavern, meeting the other players.

In general, he wasn't so thrilled with the experience. It was exciting, at first, but the novelty faded. He also explained that socializing for him took a lot of energy. He needed to change his mood and mind-set in order to engage with others. It felt like an intrusion to have this socializing world enter the private and personal space of his apartment. He did express how it was amazing that his group of friends in the game came from all across the world.

He and his girlfriend used the game to be more present with each other, but it did not make up for the needed face-to-face interaction. You can use controllers to touch each other, but Jason explained, "It's odd because your brain interprets it as real. Somebody, actually, is physically invading your personal bubble—until it's faced with incontrovertible evidence that they're not really there and you pass right through people." There were moments when they looked into each other's eyes or touched each other and when he let himself absorb the moment, it did feel like he was actually with her.

Jason explained to me the concept of "uncanny valley," when I asked him about the future of VR. It means that the closer the simulation gets to reality, the more noticeable the difference, so it becomes eerie and uncomfortable. That's where he sees an issue with wearables. He had several warnings about attempting VR in a relationship:

1. It's expensive, so be aware of cost and remember you have to buy two controllers.

2. The novelty can wear off quickly. Since the games are in still in the early stages of development, there is not much to do in them.

3. The setup is a pain. You have to calibrate your room by walking around it, in order to get the game to work. It is a frustrating process and the game is not clear about how long the process takes.

4. When you are in different time zones, there is not much time to actually connect. Sometimes it feels like a waste to use that precious time setting up the game.

All in all, he says "be open-minded, go interact with people, try it out, and you never know what can happen."

Jason and his ex-girlfriend are a perfect example of a couple who was unsure how trying a new tech product could affect their relationship. In the end, she was more excited about the game than Jason was, but he does not regret trying a new, unique experience. His story mimics my feelings about the future of tech and LDR. It's exciting, but also a bit nerve-wracking, to imagine the possibilities.

SUMMARY

There are certainly several creative and fun approaches to maintaining an LDR. The challenge of geographical separation can be seen as an opportunity for relationships to develop rather than stagnate. Prior to any separation, exploring the potential impact and communication expectations may help mitigate the distress of physical distance. If you decide to embark on an LDR, figure out prior to separation when you will be able to reconnect face-to-face. It is also helpful if partners can accept or agree on when the long-distance phase will come to an end. That way, the stress that sometimes comes with an LDR is not seen as eternal.

Discuss with one another what techniques you will utilize during the separation to enhance your relationship. Are you open to trying new products? How often do you plan to check in with one another? What type of communication platform are you willing to use? Plans can also be adapted over time, depending on schedules and responsibilities. The key is consistent and honest communication. As the research indicated, continuing to self-disclose is the key in building intimacy in an LDR. Regardless of whether you disclose through text message, Facetime, or on a call, the act of sharing will strengthen your emotional bond with your partner.

Be true to yourself and with your partner if you are open to an LDR. Some individuals need that physical closeness to feel loved and secure. Other people yearn for independence and therefore thrive in LDRs. It is better to be forthcoming than to place yourself in a situation that is uncomfortable and unsustaining.

Chapter 9

CHOICES, CHOICES, CHOICES

CASE STUDY: PARADOX OF CHOICE

Shaun, a 26-year-old employed sales manager in Boston, felt accomplished in his career. His management role gave him a sense of responsibility as well as a relatively flexible schedule. In addition to feeling vocationally satisfied, Shaun enjoyed many substantial friendships. However, he yearned for an intimate, long-term partner. He was unsuccessful in meeting people through friends or business events and decided to join dating apps with the primary goal of meeting a long-term partner. Although initially skeptical about connecting with someone through this channel, he was determined to try. He was intrigued with the accessibility of dating apps, and he felt he had thoroughly exhausted his current social sphere.

He quickly progressed to playing the swiping game (continuously swiping for matches). Late one night, he swiped and matched with a woman named Amanda. He looked closer at her profile and saw that she was an attractive, five-foot, three-inch blonde woman, who loved country music, hiking, and eating cheeseburgers (at least that's what he saw on her profile). His attitude about the app transformed as she appeared to share his interests and fulfill many of his physical preferences. She responded to his messaging, and after three days of conversation through the app, he asked for her number. Through texting, he asked her out for drinks.

Shaun was pleasantly surprised that Amanda looked even better than the pictures presented on her profile. They had a great date and proceeded to date for six months. However, Shaun did not delete the dating apps from his phone. Although he spent most of his free nights with Amanda and wasn't actively seeking anyone else, he found himself mindlessly swiping through the dating apps. Sometimes, through the apps, he engaged in conversations with women who sparked his attention. Since he never met up with any of the women in person, it did not occur to him that it would interfere with his developing relationship with Amanda.

One night, while lying in bed, Amanda brought up the topic of exclusivity. Shaun was not exactly surprised but was unsure of his feelings. He questioned his hesitation, since Amanda possessed all the qualities and characteristics he had never imagined being able to find in one person. However, he had this feeling he was not ready to stop looking. He reassured her that he was not seeing anyone else, which provided her with relief. After articulating this, Shaun felt guilty and realized his continued swiping had more significance than he previously attributed to the behavior.

The next day he had lunch with friends who described single life in glowing terms. This caused him to feel unsettled and troubled, so Shaun revisited his dating apps. Unsure of his intention, he felt the desire to check out other women. He swiped for five minutes, looking at different profiles of women. Seeing all these women made him more confused about his future with Amanda. He closed his eyes for a few minutes and thought about his relationship with Amanda. The past six months were incredible. They had a great sex life; shared meaningful conversations; and enjoyed numerous concerts, weekend getaways, and casual date nights. There was nothing specifically wrong with their relationship, and he definitely saw potential for a long-term relationship. However, he wondered how he could fully commit when there were so many other possibilities *right there* on his phone, directly in front of him. Would he regret ending an incredible relationship to pursue the unknown? What if he commits to Amanda and misses out on something potentially "better?"

The stress and pressure to make a decision weighed heavily on Shaun. He went back and forth in his mind, exploring different scenarios and outcomes. He tried asking advice from his friends, but he seemed to get a range of responses. It did not help that his mother was constantly pressuring him to settle down. He also attempted to visualize the conversation with Amanda, but that only caused further anxiety. Finally, when he could no longer deal with his indecisiveness, he decided to seek therapy. He knew his parents' marriage affected his ability to commit and that eventually he would have to explore those insecurities. His situation with Amanda motivated him to finally make the move.

ANALYSIS: THE ABUNDANCE OF CHOICES

Before cell phones or the Internet existed, the pool of potential mates was limited to the individuals people met naturally or were introduced to through mutual friends. Once two people began dating, that status continued until the couple agreed to advance the relationship to the next level. If there was a question or concern, the relationship may end, followed by the parties each attempting to find someone else who was a better fit. It was certainly possible to date multiple people simultaneously; however, due to limited technology it would have been complicated and difficult to maintain. Marriage occurred at a younger age and was the assumed goal of dating relationships, so couples didn't typically stretch out their courtship indefinitely. The decision to advance their relationship to the next level happened relatively quickly for couples in earlier generations. Technology has also allowed us to be transient and mobile, growing our networks, while communities used to be much more constant and intimate. In pre-Internet days, the whole community was often aware of who was dating whom. Couples met at local settings or one member (usually the woman) was picked up at home, making the entire dating process more conspicuous. According to Andrew Hess, who writes for Christian Mingle, "People are connecting from across the country and around the world. Gone are the days when most married couples grew up in the same county."[1]

Logistically, dating was different because most initial contacts were in person. People had to put the effort into charming their potential partner by utilizing interpersonal skills and trying to woo the other. Now, technology has increased the ease of not only finding, but also courting partners. It is possible to look for potential mates while in school, in your pajamas, or even while on a boring date with someone else. The perception of limitless choices may lead people to fear remaining committed and monogamous. Regardless of the level of intimacy and emotional connection, one may feel there could be someone else out there for them. "Out there" no longer refers to the people you meet through your friends or business partners. "Out there" now refers to the infinite possibilities the Internet has to offer. Shaun's friends reminded him of the world "out there."

Shaun cared deeply for Amanda and saw potential in their future. She had the characteristics of someone he wanted to be with long-term. Not only was he physically attracted to her, but genuinely enjoyed spending time with her. He did not specifically feel a need to meet up with other girls through the app, but feared closing that door completely. It is natural to notice attractive people on the street and to develop "crushes" on people who casually pass through your life. The difference in today's dating world is that these apps and sites give you the impression that there are unlimited options and therefore you don't have to settle down so quickly. The possibilities are endless, and the chance to meet someone else incredible is only a swipe away.

RESEARCH: THE PARADOX OF CHOICE

Having too many choices in general can be debilitating, even on the most simplistic level. For instance, picture yourself trying to choose what you want to have for dinner. There are sushi, pasta, Thai, Chinese, and the list goes on. So, how do you choose? Moreover, once you do choose, how do you stay confident with your decision? This is why I, like so many others, become overwhelmed in department stores. Imagine you are standing at one clothing rack, staring at a nice, soft T-shirt, while your eyes start to drift to the rack to your right with the black overalls draped over the top. Next thing you know, you have moved on and forgotten about the T-shirt that you probably needed and are staring at the cute overalls that will be perfect for summer six months away.

Multiple studies have demonstrated that excessive choice can produce "choice paralysis," but also that it can reduce people's satisfaction with their decisions, even if they made good ones. Many of these studies looked at the likelihood of individuals purchasing products at grocery stores when offered more options of a certain item. Barry Schwartz, author of *The Paradox of Choice: Why More Is Less*, explains at what point choice—the hallmark of individual freedom and self-determination that we so cherish—becomes detrimental to our psychological and emotional well-being.[2] He also shows how our obsession with alternatives encourages us to seek what may make us feel worse.

According to Schwartz, more choices require increased time and effort and can lead to anxiety, regret, excessively high expectations, and self-blame if the decided-upon choice does not work out. It is understandable that self-blame tends to be harsher when there were originally multiple selections possible, because you only have yourself to blame for going in a certain direction. Even when people make the best determination possible at a given time, there runs a risk of the result being one that was unsatisfying. Schwartz explains, "When the number of available options is small, these costs are negligible, but the costs grow with the number of options. Eventually, each new option makes us feel worse off than we did before."[3]

Sociologist Eric Klinenberg, who teamed up with Aziz Ansari to write *Modern Romance*, explains how modern dating can drive people crazy due to the overwhelming amount of choices provided by the dating apps.[4] He asserts this is a main reason why dating apps are limiting the amount of people that members can speak to or match with on a given day. According to Ansari, "It's easy to find and get the best, so why not do it? If you are in a big city or on an online-dating site, you are now comparing your potential partners not just to other potential partners but rather to an idealized person to whom no one could measure up. But people don't always know what they're looking for in a soul mate, unlike when they're picking something easier, like laundry detergent."[5]

I spoke to dating app JSwipe founder David Yarus about the paradox of choice.[6] He agreed that having unlimited choices can become an issue and that he himself struggles daily with indecisiveness. According to Yarus, although the apps do provide more partner choices for members, it is up to each individual to practice discipline. He went on to express the need for a dating app that not only provides choices but also teaches you how to date. He feels that this would help eliminate certain prospective matches and help you find the right partner. Brian Dunham, founder of OhMiBod, a company that manufactures and sells vibrators, agreed and said that the dating apps are not the issues.[7] Individuals need to have the dating skills and confidence to progress their relationships after meeting through the apps. The apps should only be a way to reach your destination faster.

In describing the paradox of choice phenomenon as it relates to dating, Yarus stated (personal communication):

> It's really real, the more you swipe, the more you get matches, and the more you get matches, the more confusing it will be. But it is, like everything else in life, a tool that you wield the power of. You can either use it effectively, use it strategically, and use it responsibly, which will lead you to find someone great and quickly, or you can distract yourself into utter confusion and not be able to settle down at all.

Based on the research, it is not surprising that Shaun felt confused about the decision to commit fully to Amanda. In essence, this trend is just an extension of the "grass is always greener on the other side" thought process. It is natural to compare to others, to imagine what else is out there, and to assume it is perhaps better than what you have. However, when you add an abundance of choices to that thought process, it is no wonder why Shaun felt stressed and doubtful. Shaun's success in his career was also based upon his ability to consider multiple options prior to making a decision. He prided himself at work at being able to weigh multiple factors, to quickly research potential avenues, and to make decisions based on that analysis. Although he acknowledged some errors of judgment at work, these were not irrevocable, and he was able to return to his original crossroads and reconsider. In relationships, however, he felt more pressured and fearful that whatever decision he made would have irreversible consequences. The knowledge that there were so many other potential partners that he hadn't even explored fully weighed on him.

THERAPY: SO WHAT NOW?

Shaun was distraught. He knew he had to reach some sort of conclusion before seeing Amanda again. After all, he cared for her and did not want to string her along or be dishonest about speaking with other women. He continually vacillated between making a commitment to Amanda or keeping his options open. He described in session that he had created a list of pros and cons in his head, which fluctuated constantly and created further indecisiveness.

Shaun needed to not only practice discipline, as Yarus stated; he also needed to shift his mind-set regarding dating. After all, Amanda wasn't proposing or asking him to commit for eternity. Shaun and Amanda were still in the process of getting to know each other. When Shaun slowed down and focused on the present phase with Amanda, he was hopeful. Shaun's involvement with the dating app might have contributed to his confusion. If they had just met through friends, gone out a few months and decided only to see each other for a while, my guess is he would have been completely on board. His ambivalence never seemed to be about Amanda or their relationship. The prospect of seeing her that week made him feel happy. He had not attempted to commit to Amanda without side conversations and therefore did not know what that would feel like. Similar to the concept of "cushioning," which I will discuss in Chapter 10, having partners on the backburner reduces the feeling of vulnerability. Committing only to Amanda would feel different, but it was impossible to know exactly how without jumping in completely.

Part of treatment is also reducing temptation. Some individuals in my focus groups mentioned deleting the apps from their phones but keeping their accounts active. That is like taking chocolate off your counter and putting it high up on a cabinet shelf. If you want it, you'll get to it, and eat it. If you truly want to eliminate the compulsion to swipe and see what is out there, you need to delete your account entirely. Worst-case scenario, you can create another one in the future. This intervention is effective for people who had the insight to recognize the antecedents of their behavior and express motivation to change.

Shaun was especially susceptible to becoming overwhelmed with options that had no certainties. He felt that his perfectionism at work led him to professional success. In his career, he utilized concrete logic and numbers when exploring options and making decisions. This enabled him to feel confident that he came to the correct determination. Relying on emotions to make a decision made him feel uneasy, which ironically would have helped him choose a direction.

For Shaun, dating apps were his main trigger. Unfortunately, the fact that "it worked" and enabled him to find Amanda further reinforced his obsession to investigate more matches. However, apps were not the only forms of temptation on social media. Facebook, Instagram, and Snapchat (and I'm sure something else by the time this book comes out) all display images in some form of good-looking people. You can follow certain accounts or browse photos of anyone you find attractive. In order to be disciplined, it is first essential to become aware of your own triggers. Which forms of temptations are just fun and entertaining, and which forms cause your mind to stray into a world of doubt and angst?

THERAPY: EXPLORING HIS VULNERABILITIES

Shaun did not have a great role model for healthy relationships. His parents, although still married, were in a volatile relationship. Both parents had affairs throughout the marriage. At one point, they separated for a few months but ended up back together and Shaun could not understand why. He saw relationships ending up in one of two ways: either settling and complacency or infidelity and destruction. He also observed his friends getting engaged, and inferred that they did not seem particularly satisfied in their relationships. To protect himself from ending up discontented, he remained detached in his relationships. His association with vulnerability was setting yourself up for a failed or unfulfilling relationship.

His previous relationships ended after a few months. He blamed those endings on being too preoccupied with work and advancing his career. As he reflected on those relationships, he realized that he never fully invested himself. Mainly, he never really wanted to fully invest himself. At the time, he thought he was giving adequate energy and attention to his partners. In reality, the wall he preemptively placed between him and his partners would never allow him to move forward in the relationship. According to Brown, "In a world where scarcity and shame dominate and feeling afraid has become second nature, vulnerability is subversive. Uncomfortable. It's even a little dangerous at times. And, without question, putting ourselves out there means there's a far greater risk of feeling hurt."[8]

Shaun discovered his patterns and identified his fear of vulnerability. He also acknowledged how this pattern would not allow him to accomplish his goal to marry and have a family. He did not want to run away from his relationship with Amanda but also was unsure how to be vulnerable. He had never disclosed his feelings about his parents with a partner. He had also never let his guard down and knew the risk he would have to take by doing so. We also explored in therapy the positive outcomes of becoming vulnerable. Sometimes, being vulnerable is only described alongside fear. However, learning how to be vulnerable also requires strength and perseverance. Although exposing his vulnerability to Amanda would be difficult, it would also be rewarding. Shaun would experience a new, unfamiliar side of himself that he might actually enjoy.

RESEARCH: SLOW LOVE

It is no secret that Millennials are marrying and starting families later in life. According to Pew Social Trends, "Millennials are significantly less likely to be married than previous generations in their 20s. By 2016, the median age at first marriage had reached its highest point on record: 29.5 years for men and 27.4 years for women."[9] Previous generations were typically married with children at the same age that newer generations are having their first Tinder (a dating app) date.

One major reason for this trend is financial situations. For logistical purposes, Millennials want to feel stable in their careers and financial situation before marrying and starting a family. However, concurrently, the percentage of 18- to 24-year-olds who use online dating have almost tripled in recent years, from 10 percent in 2013 to 27 percent in 2016. Mobile dating apps are driving much of this increase: 22 percent of 18- to 24-year-olds now report using mobile dating apps, up from just 5 percent in 2013.[10] It is not a coincidence these trends are happening simultaneously. It is clear that due to the abundance of choices and the ease of meeting online, Millennials want to be more secure in their decision of a life-long partner.

This is not necessarily problematic. According to biological anthropologist Helen Fisher, young daters are practicing "slow love."[11] She explains that the younger generations are taking their time to sleep around, have friends with benefits, or live with their partners before they commit to marriage. This is backed up by a General Social Survey of 33,000 U.S. adults, conducted by San Diego State University psychologist Jean Twenge and her colleagues, which found that premarital sex has become more socially accepted over the years.[12] The percentage of survey respondents who viewed premarital sex as "not wrong at all" grew from about 29 percent in the 1970s to 58 percent by 2012. Generally, during the past decade, Americans tended to have more sexual partners, were more likely to have casual sex, and were more accepting of premarital sex, compared to the 1970s and 1980s.[13]

Fisher feels that this notion of "slow love" is the opposite of recklessness. If anything, Millennials want to be more confident in whom they marry. Ms. Fisher believes that marriage will continue because humans still crave attachment and love, and fear being alone. Therefore, the only difference is that the process is slower and the tactics of meeting people have changed.

RESEARCH: THE DATING APOCALYPSE

Nancy Jo Sales wrote an article entitled "The Dating Apocalypse," which appeared in *Vanity Fair* in 2015.[14] Sales quoted both men and women who expressed various reasons for employing dating apps. Her interviewees, in their 20s, described their frustration with dating apps. They also said they felt dating no longer felt romantic because of the apps. For example, one man stated, "You can't be stuck in one lane. . . . There's always something better." Another said, "If you had a reservation somewhere and then a table at Per Se opened up, you'd want to go there." Justin McLeod, founder of the dating app Hinge, responded to this article by rebranding their app to refocus on the importance of meeting people for relationship purposes. They changed their URL to reflect this new brand: TheDatingApocalyse.com. They do not believe that dating apps necessarily lead to a dating apocalypse but could be a great way to form meaningful relationships. The Hinge website states, "Dating apps have become a game, and with every swipe we've all moved further from the real connections that we crave. So we built something better. The new Hinge is redesigned for relationships. It's a members-only community for people looking to get past the games and find something real."[15]

Their promotion video evokes that feeling of loneliness that arises when constantly swiping. The swiping becomes a game, where you win by matching with as many people as possible instead of forming a relationship. This reflects the notion that, given the abundance of choices on apps, you might end up with nothing.

Regardless of your perception or opinion of dating apps, it is clear that modern dating requires a new set of communication skills and mind-set. When trends in dating evolve, humans need to develop new techniques and interpersonal competence to navigate and succeed. Touchpoint founder Jared Weiss realized this need and monopolized on this space. He created a town hall in New York City, where people gather to talk about how to date and have sex in the modern world. Touchpoint has now spread to Miami, San Francisco, and Mexico City.

According to their mission statement, "We believe that when it comes to matters of the heart, often there are no questions and answers, only questions and ideas. At Touchpoint, all ideas are welcome. Our mission is to empower people to be their best in bed, in love, and in life."[16] Weiss explained to me how Touchpoint began when he and a few friends met together to discuss the difficulties of dating and mating in a techno-driven world.[17] Soon, a small group get-together turned into a monthly event. People want a space to vent, a space to share ideas, and a space to get tips and tools on how to navigate this complicated arena. Prior to meeting, attendees are allowed to submit questions for the group to discuss. The group then picks questions that are most interesting. This community is a great way to share in the hardships of dating and attendees walk away with new friends and confidence.

RESEARCH: SO . . . IS LESS, MORE?

According to Schwartz, less is definitely more. He concluded that too many options can feel overwhelming and cause us to choose nothing. Daniel Mochon, writer and author of "Single-Option Aversion" feels very differently.[18]

In order to understand "single-option aversion," think about walking into Bed Bath & Beyond. I specifically bring up this store because they sell awesome and "cool" stuff that you just *need* to have. Anyway, imagine you spot this amazing grilled cheese maker. Who doesn't want that? You imagine yourself late at night, watching a movie, and you get the munchies. The only thing that could make the night better is a cheesy sandwich. So, as you stand there in Bed Bath & Beyond, you decide you need the grilled cheese maker. You look at the price, and you see it costs $99.99. Wow!! That is an expensive grilled cheese maker. The fantasy of eating grilled cheese while watching *Criminal Minds* slowly fades away, and you don't purchase the product.

Now, let's redo this entire scenario, but now you see three different grilled cheese makers sitting side by side. They look a little different but seem to accomplish the same goal. One grilled cheese maker is selling for $189, the second one sells for $147, and the third one for $99.99. In this scenario, the $99.99 option doesn't sound so bad, and you decide to buy it, assuming you are getting a great deal. Mochon says there are a few reasons this occurs. The first is that you have no idea what a grilled cheese maker is supposed to cost. All you have are the three models in front of you and your beautiful fantasy of eating late-night grilled cheese. In your mind, you are actually being cost-conscious by not purchasing the expensive models.

However, another reason, according to Mochon, is that you are incredibly reluctant to buy certain items—especially expensive items—when only one option is presented. He found that people like having multiple items to compare. When he offered DVD players to participants in one study, just 9 percent said they would buy a Sony model when it was the only option. When paired with a Philips DVD player, the number went up to 32 percent. The mere presence of options quadrupled willingness to buy. Mochon replicated the finding with TVs and donations. He suggests that having multiple options makes us more certain about our final choice.

Mochon said, "Even if consumers can find an option that they like, they may be unwilling to purchase it without considering other similar options first."[19] That's why Best Buy doesn't offer two television sets or two cameras. It offers hundreds. It's why Starbucks and Whole Foods aren't irrational to give their shoppers a bounty of options. Sometimes, choices can paralyze us with anxiety and exhaust us. Other times, choices reduce anxiety by making us feel like we've searched exhaustively—and now we're ready to buy.

So what does buying a grilled cheese maker have to do with dating? If you take the advice of Machon, it is not necessarily a best practice to date just one person or have only one option right from the get go. However, according to Schwartz, having too many options is exhausting, frustrating, and detrimental in finding a partner. So where does that leave you? I think it's safe to say that there is healthy compromise. That compromise can look different for each individual depending on his or her specific situation and what type of relationship he or she is seeking. Make sure you are comfortable, secure, and aware of your intentions of dating numerous partners simultaneously. Be mindful of how it impacts your emotions and if it exacerbates or alleviates your anxiety.

IMPLICATIONS FOR THERAPISTS: EXPLORING PARADOX OF CHOICE

When clients are on dating app, I sometimes look at their profile with them. Are they accurately presenting themselves? Do they have good insight as to how they come across? Who are they looking for? If they appear obsessed with the app, meaning they continuously check it and their emotions are completely dependent on whether or not there is a match, we explore their need for validation. Why is receiving a match the only indication of their worth?

Dating apps can be a positive way to enable clients, especially those who feel socially stagnant, to meet new people and actively pursue their goals. If they become overwhelmed with the options available, use this opportunity to explore how they set priorities and how they make decisions. Sometimes people are so afraid to make a choice because a better one will be around the corner. This will not just be manifested in their dating search, but probably affect other aspects of their life. Determining which dating app they should utilize could be explored through conducting research. This is a transferrable skill to other life choices.

Commitment can be unnerving. When clients reports that the reason they cannot commit is the paradox of choice, avoid scrutinizing that phenomenon and encourage them to sit with their fear of commitment. What is scary? What are they afraid of losing? Is this a manifestation of fear of vulnerability? In this case, the propensity of choices is defensive, distracting the client from examining their attitudes toward long-term allegiances.

IMPLICATIONS FOR THERAPISTS: ADVICE TO CLIENTS

When clients face fear of commitment and are overly focused on the paradox of choice, interventions to facilitate slowing down are beneficial. At times, people become too future-oriented and dating apps can reinforce this perspective. Encouraging clients to focus on the present by guiding them on a realistic journey toward fulfillment can help ease some of the anxiety. Offering the following pieces of advice in a therapeutic setting can promote growth, reflection, and informed decision making.

1. **Breathe and relax.** If the body does not feel healthy, neither does the mind. Getting sleep, exercising, meditating, and eating healthy are just some of the ways to improve health. Ultimately, if we feel better, we can make better choices. Clients can map out a plan of how they will incorporate these healthy practices into their lives.

2. **Stay in the moment.** There are many reasons why people become obsessed about the future. They want to know what outcomes will result from their actions in 5,

10, or 15 years. Often clients tell me how they wish they had a crystal ball to help them make decisions. In reality, there is no possible way to predict the future. Our choices can only be based on our emotions and our experiences. Being thoroughly mindful of ourselves at any given point in time mitigates impulsive decision making. For example, Shaun would reflect on his relationship with Amanda. What did their relationship look like? What drove him to keep spending time with her? He would describe his feelings toward her and then express his concerns and his ambivalence to commit. Shaun needed the opportunity to sit with his current feelings. Although he tended to jump to "what if" scenarios, I would hold him to what was going on in the current moment. Jumping to assumptions about the future could also be defensive. Focusing on the ambivalence may preclude fully experiencing the present. Perhaps there were issues in the relationship that needed further exploration, but in some ways, it was easier to obsess about the future.

3. **Trust yourself.** After describing the situation, clients will ultimately reach an outcome, especially if you are utilizing solution-focused therapy. By this point, they have openly discussed their needs, goals, and values, and have therefore reached an educated decision. They need to trust their gut. Whichever decision they made was a result of the facts and feelings of the present moment. Once Shaun adequately describes the relationship, and his feelings toward Amanda, he can make a decision about whether he wants to move things forward. Based on his conversation with her, he needs to hone in on their relationship and separate that from his struggle to look elsewhere. This will allow him to make an adequate decision.

4. **Nothing has to be permanent.** Feelings can change and situations can change. Especially when you are in the early stage of a relationship, the goal is to learn about each other to determine if you found a good match. When you agree to be exclusive, you are ultimately saying that you care enough to solely explore that relationship. If there is a change in the chemistry between partners, clients will be able to adapt accordingly. This removes some of the stress of the notion of making a "life-long" commitment. Throughout the relationship, clients will work in therapy to understand the root of this fear. In the meantime, they should not avoid maintaining a positive relationship that offers them fulfillment.

SUMMARY

Dating apps can be a fun and exciting way to meet new people. Setting realistic expectations and having an open-minded attitude creates the best chance of success. Dating apps provide an additional social opportunity and a means to expand your social connections. Sometimes the connections people make through apps lead to networking opportunities for themselves or others. For example, you may meet someone who you realize is an ideal match for a friend or find someone who becomes your friend for years to come. If you are convinced you will meet your soulmate immediately, you are setting yourself up for disappointment. If that does happen, then better to be pleasantly surprised.

Dating apps should certainly not replace other forms of interpersonal communication. Try pushing yourself out of your comfort zone to engage in face-to-face conversations. Continue to go to events with your friends. Networking events are not only beneficial for making professional connections but can also establish long-term friendships and romantic relationships. Ask to be set up if you are looking for a relationship. The more avenues you try, the more likely you'll find what you are looking for. If you find yourself overwhelmed with choices to the point where no one is meeting your needs, it might be helpful to slow down and take a break from dating. Go out with friends, enjoy your hobbies, focus on your career, and work on a temporary attitude transition. This will ultimately help you figure out what you are looking for in a partner.

If you decide to utilize dating apps, remember that individuals are choosing to use them for different reasons. You can match with someone who might not be looking for a long-term relationship. Additionally, you might be dating someone who is also exploring other relationships simultaneously. Keep in mind that the person you are dating could be struggling with the paradox of choice.

Exploring your fears and vulnerabilities can promote inner growth and enhance relationships. If you find that your relationships tend to end prematurely or that you overly concern yourself with the future, try exploring this thought process in therapy. Tackling these thoughts sooner rather than later is the best way to avoid conflict and disappointment. Ruminating and anticipating conflicts may impede the development of an emotional connection.

Paradox of choice is a real phenomenon that should not be dismissed. It can be detrimental to someone's personal and professional life. Trusting your instinct, intelligence, emotions, and perspective is not always easy and sometimes requires therapeutic intervention. Competent therapists can give good feedback and help move the process along. With the right attitude, multiple choices are positive in that they allow for individuality of expression and fulfillment of needs. The trick is to be clear with yourself that you are making the best decision possible at this point in your life. When you mindfully consider your options, you give yourself the best prospect of success. We know there are no guarantees in life. Therefore, try not to get stuck on always wondering about the greener grass on the other app.

Chapter 10

GHOSTING AND CUSHIONING

CASE STUDY: GREG'S DISAPPEARANCE

Michelle, a 27-year-old female, was navigating the world of dating apps. She went on a few, entertaining dates where she saw some potential. Other dates fell on a continuum from humorous to disastrous, which made her want to crawl into a ball. She felt positive and optimistic that she would eventually meet the right person. After downloading an app that seemed to more closely address her requirements, she met Greg. Greg was 28 years old and was successfully employed in advertising. For their first date, they went to a bar for a couple of drinks and then went to a comedy club. Michelle enjoyed the date and was excited when Greg ended the night by asking to see her again later that week. Their second date was dinner at a quaint, romantic, Italian restaurant. Greg revealed to Michelle that his parents were getting divorced and that, although it was a sad time, he actually felt relieved that they would finally stop fighting. Michelle was supportive and appreciated Greg's openness. Over the next couple of weeks, Greg and Michelle continued to date each other. They enjoyed a range of experiences, including an Ed Sheeran Concert, a Ranger's Hockey Game, and a challenging hike.

The relationship seemed to be progressing, or so Michelle thought. She felt secure as Greg consistently proposed dates to get together. Although they never discussed exclusivity, Michelle also felt confident that they were focusing their energy on each other. After three weeks of dating, Michelle went away for a three-day work trip to Florida. During those three days, Greg never initiated conversation. Michelle texted him a few times to check in, and Greg responded with short answers. Michelle was concerned but assumed she was being oversensitive and perhaps reacting to being away.

When Michelle returned home, she texted Greg and asked him to come over. She offered to cook him his favorite meal (although she mentioned she would probably botch it due to her cooking skills). Greg responded, "That sounds great. I'm just super busy finishing this project for work. Let's hang later in the week." Michelle was disappointed but still felt satisfied that he wanted to see her. When Wednesday rolled around and she had not heard from Greg, she got an uneasy feeling. This was out of the norm. She was unsure if she should reach out again for fear of seeming desperate. By the time Friday approached, she felt completely out of control. She was having trouble functioning and had no appetite. Her friends became concerned for her health and forced her to reach out. After spending 10 minutes constructing the perfect text with her friends, she wrote, "I hope you were able to finish your project! I would love to see you this weekend." Greg never responded, and Michelle never heard from him again.

ANALYSIS: GHOSTING

The definition of ghosting is suddenly ending a personal relationship without explanation, withdrawing from all forms of communication. Ghosting can occur whether you have been on one date or, unfortunately and surprisingly, after months of dating. Michelle, like many victims of ghosting, felt utterly confused, enraged, and rejected. "How can we go from seeing each other multiple times per week to just suddenly not speaking?" voiced an agitated Michelle. Once ghosting occurs, questions form, thoughts arise, and feelings of uncertainty develop about yourself and about dating, in general.

Before social media was so integral to our lives, denying you received someone's call was a credible excuse for ignoring them. Now your partner can check your Instagram account and see you put a Lo-fi filter on a photo of your dog frolicking in the grass. Clearly, you are available but chose not to answer their message. Ultimately, there is no hiding. Even if you are not a social media poster, chances are your friend is, and your partner will spot you in the background of a photo getting down on the dance floor or ordering a drink at the bar. Although this trend has always been around, technology increases the possibility of the ghoster becoming discovered and the ghostee getting hurt more easily.

In Michelle's case, she felt completely distraught. She couldn't fathom how something like this was possible. She had heard of ghosting happening in other relationships but never expected to experience it herself. It was that notion that "this is something that happens to other people." Michelle's biggest complaint was the lack of closure. She felt disrespected in that Greg did not have the decency to end the relationship either in person or at least over the phone. She had no idea what he was thinking, or what went wrong, and questioned herself. She wondered if she had imagined the entire three weeks. She stated, "I feel like the last few weeks didn't happen. There is no way the same man I dated, kissed, and cared for would do this to me." She thought she had the capacity to "read" people and then found herself in a situation where she had misjudged someone entirely.

There are multiple factors that result in ghosting. Regardless of these reasons, the ghoster walks away from the relationship leaving the ghostee feeling angry, resentful, and insecure. Since ghosting also confuses the one who is left, many clients inquire as to why people ghost. So I constructed a brief summary of the main explanations.

ANALYSIS: WHY PEOPLE GHOST

1. They Met Someone Else

With modern dating, especially with the use of dating apps, the chance that people are dating multiple people is high. Although you might feel confident in your relationship, it is possible that your partner is assessing other relationships simultaneously. Therefore, at a certain point, your partner might decide he or she feels more strongly about someone else. Before you know it, your partner disappears without any word, leaving you in a state of confusion. As I discussed in the previous chapter, the abundance of choices has consequences and dating apps make it easier to gauge multiple partners. However, this does not excuse the disrespect of not being open and honest throughout the process.

2. Don't Know What to Say

When queried about why they ghosted, some clients simply explained, "I did not know what to say." A short, blunt, but honest answer. They explained that they couldn't construct an appropriate message they felt comfortable sending. I asked, "Why not just be honest?" They replied that if they were honest, it would be hurtful. If they made up an excuse, they would feel guilty. Many of them said they spent some time thinking about potential texts, before deciding they would rather walk away from the situation entirely. Better to not text at all than to craft an awkward message, right? This leads perfectly into the next reason for ghosting: avoiding confrontation.

3. Avoiding Confrontation and Discomfort

It is conceivable that the ghoster has a narcissistic and/or avoidant personality disorder, unable to truly care about the impact ghosting/abandonment has on the other. The ghostee needs to consider his or her attraction to this personality type especially if this has occurred more than once. According to Sarah Louise Ryan, a relationship expert, "the person doing the ghosting would much rather consider their own emotional/physical discomfort above integrity, emotional intelligence and compassion for the other party in the relationship."[1] The individual who ghosts is therefore too self-absorbed with his or her own experience to put himself or herself in the place of the other.

However, some people avoid confrontation in all their relationships and tend to flee when they feel this discomfort. Inevitably, they will have a disagreement with a partner and, rather than work through it, prematurely terminate the relationship. Circumventing a tense discussion becomes easier with technology. The individual makes a conscious choice to reduce his or her own anxiety rather than provide his or her partner with closure.

4.   Scared about the Future

Clients have also shared with me that they ghost when they feel their partner is moving too quickly in the relationship. They feel pressured when exclusivity or engagement is mentioned. The concept of commitment generates anxiety that causes them to retreat from the relationship. I wondered aloud why they did not just voice this concern with their partner. These clients described difficulty articulating these feelings. They struggled to find words that communicated their trepidation because they had yet to fully understand the foundation of the issue. Attempting to avoid the confrontation, they preferred withdrawing rather than being direct and honest.

These clients had significant insecurities that interfered with their ability to mature emotionally and thus engage in an intimate relationship. If they acknowledged these concerns with their partners, they would have the potential to sort through any sort of misunderstandings or expectations of the relationship. This would actually provide them an opportunity to develop a positive relationship that involves forthright communication. Instead, they chose to abandon the relationship, allow their fears to control them, and deny their partner the right to understand what went wrong.

5.   The Accidental Ghoster

After reading the beginning of this chapter, you might think to yourself: *Have I ever ghosted anyone?* If you go on dating apps, there is a chance that you may have inadvertently ghosted someone. With the abundance of partner choices on top of everyday distractions, it is easy to lose track of a casual conversation in a dating app.

Smartphones and technology can actually encourage ghosting. Caller ID enables someone to see the caller, so there are no accidental pickups. In the past, someone called a home phone and if a roommate or family member answered, the message got through or at least you made contact. Now it is possible to completely ignore the efforts of another to get in touch with you. It is also easier to delay confrontation with text. Greg, for example, postponed meeting with Michelle twice. If this was a voice call, it may have been more difficult for him to lie or hide the fact that he really did not want to see her again.

6.   The App Ghoster

Another interesting type of ghosting is the *app ghoster.* Consider Julie, an experienced *app ghoster.* Julie goes on a dating app and proceeds to message and chat with multiple suitors. After texting with one specific suitor named Brian, she decides she is no longer interested and finds the other potentials more intriguing. Brian comes across as boring and brought up his mom and dog one too many times. Therefore, Brian is "out." Julie does not feel a need to let him know since they have only chatted a few times, which in her mind does not warrant a "breakup." Ignoring him would not suffice because his picture comes up when he contacts her. The simplest way to deal with this is for Julie to delete the entire conversation and, consequently, Brian as a match.

Brian, on the other hand, does not typically chat with many girls simultaneously on the app. He finds it confusing and would rather focus on one conversation at a time. He sees Julie as a potential match, in that she is close to her family, loves sports, is certainly attractive (at least in her pictures), and has a sarcastic sense of humor (which was a requirement for him). They chatted almost daily, and he was feeling satisfied enough with their conversations to ask her on a date. He opens the app and can't find their conversation. He scrolls down through previous conversations thinking maybe there was a glitch and the conversation got moved. Confused and annoyed when he still can't find their conversation, he opens the app website, goes to the FAQ section, and sees *One of My Matches Disappeared.* He reads the response given:

> It sounds like that person either unmatched you or deleted their account. Try logging out and logging back in just to be sure. Tap the icon on the top left-hand corner of the main screen, select "Settings" or "App Setting," scroll down and hit "Logout," then log back in.

Following the directions, Brian logs out and logs back in. His thread of exchanges with Julie is still missing. Although he never met Julie, Brian regrets not asking for her cell number. He will never know for sure if Julie intentionally deleted him, but he wishes he could at least find out what went wrong. Brian will certainly recover since he was not emotionally attached to Julie and certainly had no physical or intimate connection. This relatively new circumstance of sudden, complete disconnect leaves people, at a minimum, disconcerted. Understandably rattled, Brian moves on, but not knowing if this was a rejection or error further increases the frustration. While conducting focus groups and interviews for this book, I asked participants about their experiences with ghosting. One participant I interviewed described the impact of having her communication with a potential partner deleted. She felt a vindictiveness because someone actively "deleted" her rather than simply ending or even ignoring continual conversation.

ANALYSIS: WHO GETS GHOSTED?

Ghosting can happen to anyone who attempts to put himself or herself out there emotionally. There is no shame in being ghosted. You are not to blame for being abandoned by a suitor. However, if it has happened to you multiple times, you might want to take a deeper look at the patterns of your relationships. Sometimes people who are ghosted frequently realize that they are not accurately communicating their thoughts and feelings through text. In person, people relay expression through their body language, eye contact, and other nonverbal cues.

After reading the six reasons why people ghost, perhaps you can gain some clarity into why this might have happened to you in your past relationships. This does not mean that you necessarily have to change your entire persona and it certainly does not justify the behavior of your partner. However, it can be helpful to learn and grow from your experiences. Were there signs that you missed throughout the dating experience that would give any indication that something was wrong? Was there a part of you that worried about the relationship progressing but chose to ignore those signs? Sometimes asking for feedback can also be a way to gain clarity about what went wrong. If you are told you presented yourself in a certain way that is distressing and confusing to you, perhaps you need to become more self-aware of your language choices and actions.

I spoke to psychiatrist Almas Nazir, who has been treating women in their 20s and 30s who indicate they are victims of ghosting.[2] I asked if she saw any trends among these women. She explained that women who have been ghosted repeatedly seem to go after men who are clearly disinterested, noncommittal, or avoidant. She works with these patients on understanding why they are pursuing the "bad boys" or the "cool guys," instead of men who treat them nicely, attentively, and are able to emotionally commit. This is a general pattern that Nazir tends to see in her office and does not represent the population as a whole. However, reflecting on your previous relationships can help you learn about the types of partners you are seeking and ascertain if a pattern needs to be broken.

RESEARCH: GHOSTING BEHAVIOR

Nora Crotty, writer for Elle.com, conducted a survey of 185 people, 120 women and 65 men on their dating and breakup habits. She found that 13.64 percent of men have been ghosted, whereas 16.67 percent of men have ghosted partners and that 26.67 percent of women have been ghosted while 24.17 percent have ghosted their partners. [3]

The study clearly shows that ghosting is not a gendered phenomenon. Both males and females can be both victims and perpetrators of ghosting. That's because both males and females are humans and therefore get anxious, worried, and overthink. They react by bolting to avoid feeling vulnerable or to avoid confronting a partner.

Ghosting as a means to end a relationship leads to a plethora of reactions because it creates the ultimate scenario of ambiguity. Should you be worried? What if he's are hurt and lying in a hospital bed somewhere? Should you be upset? Maybe she is just a little busy and will be calling you at any moment. You do not know how to react because it is unclear what has happened and there are so many possibilities.

Within any regulatory system, there must be mechanisms that allow for the assessment of current needs (e.g., blood sugar levels and food needs) or some type of signal when the needs are unmet (e.g., the state of feeling hungry). Staying connected to others is so important to our survival. Maslow considered the state of belonging to be a need only surpassed by safety and basic physiological needs.[4] Our brains have evolved to have a social monitoring system (SMS) to monitor the environment for cues so that we know how to respond in social situations. Social cues allow us to regulate our own behavior accordingly. For example, when you see an eye roll, you know that what you said is being judged or criticized. With the advent of texting, we forgo these types of cues and increase our reliance on assumptions. We need to develop a different set of monitoring behavior. For example, noticing that you are constantly initiating a text or always the one responding quickly should be a red flag. If you are mindful of these cues, the blindsided experience of being ghosted may be prevented.

The *New York Times* surveyed individuals who were brave enough to reveal themselves as ghosters. Some self-identified ghosters explain that, due to dating apps, there is "a myriad supply of anonymous suitors."[5] Although the choices are endless, there's only a limited amount of time and energy available to devote to each potential partner. Therefore, if one person doesn't make the cut, it is way easier to move onto the next instead of crafting a goodbye message. According to one of the ghosters, "Ghosting is so tantalizingly easy, it makes the 'It's not you, it's me' breakup seem like rocket science."

Another individual I interviewed discussed how he ghosted to avert experiencing himself as "the bad guy." He avoided being the person who ended the relationship because he truly felt anguish if caused another to feel pain. Although his reasoning was understandable, he didn't realize that the rejection was still experienced, and was in fact intensified, because of his avoidance. He recognized that it was a disingenuous way of ending a relationship. However, the relationship was relatively short-lived, and he did not have a plausible explanation for terminating it. He acknowledged that saying nothing and disappearing was the "easy way out," especially since articulating his ambiguity seemed more of a struggle than the relationship warranted. Since he really did not have a specific reason to end the relationship, it seemed easier to say nothing.

THERAPY: INCREASING SELF-CONFIDENCE

When Michelle initially presented for therapy, she wanted to hear specifically why I thought Greg ghosted her. Similar to experiencing a loss or trauma, the process of recovering from being ghosted happens in stages. At this point, Michelle was at Stage One: feeling hurt, confused, and shocked. This period mimics the stage of denial when you suffer a loss, in that you cannot fathom that something of that nature could have occurred. She explained her dates in detail, becoming increasingly frustrated and agitated as she reflected on those memorable weeks. Phrases such as "Can you believe it!?" and "This just makes no sense" were consistently repeated.

I explained that how there are multiple reasons why someone would ghost and that it was impossible to explicitly know Greg's rationale. Once she was given validation and sufficient time to vent, she entered Stage Two: anger. Statements such as "Who does she think she is?" or "Is he kidding? I am way too good for him" can be heard during this phase.

After a couple of sessions processing, over-analyzing, and expressing resentment, Michelle entered Stage Three: self-blame. She expressed that, as much as she wanted to be mad at Greg, she couldn't help but look inward and blame herself. After all, "Clearly something was wrong with me if he suddenly felt a need to disappear." She convinced herself that she was either not good enough for him or that she somehow scared him away. She reflected back on all their previous conversations, especially right before she embarked on her trip, but couldn't pinpoint anything specifically that would cause Greg to retreat. This was an important phase as it was essential for Michelle to understand it was *not her fault*. Regardless of what she texted before, during, or after her trip, Greg would have ghosted. The common trend is for people to contemplate whether they said or did the wrong thing to specifically trigger the ghosting. Ghosters ghost. It is how they end relationships. Blaming yourself or lingering on one specific word that you muttered or action that you took is not only pointless but also inconsequential.

Prior to his disappearance, Greg made Michelle feel special and cared for with his words and actions. She repeatedly expressed how he made her feel desired, smart, and safe. He regularly complimented her and outwardly demonstrated his attraction for her with public displays of affection. She found herself doubting not only the validity of his feelings but also the truth of those words of affirmation. The lack of closure on top of rejection threw her into a whirlwind of self-doubt and deprecation.

We delved into her sense of self, uncovering her personal strengths and weaknesses. She took a few moments to envision herself prior to the relationship. She stated, "I was a confident person, a leader in both my workplace and amongst my friends. I always saw myself as somewhat attractive, motivated, and outgoing." Prior to dating Greg, she felt secure that she was a good catch and deserved a partner with similar aspirations and values. Michelle was really thrown off by this experience as it deeply affected her sense of self.

Before working on her self-esteem, I made sure to give Michelle a chance to vent and a space to feel hurt and angry. After all, she had experienced a loss and deserved a grieving period. After a sufficient length of time reflecting on her relationship, she was ready to attempt a range of techniques to move past the relationship. She wrote down her strengths and posted them around her apartment. She even had some of her closest friends write some notes she could read whenever she felt insecure. She also destroyed all memories of Greg, by cutting up concert tickets, deleting pictures, and erasing his number from her phone. Once Greg was removed from sight, she was able to focus on herself and her personal needs. Michelle finally reached Stage Four: "f*** you. I'm amazing." Michelle was ready to move on from the relationship.

Since this was Michelle's first time being ghosted, it did not seem necessary to institute major behavioral changes. However, if this happens more than once and/or the client feels leery of reentering the dating world, I would suggest the next relationship be less tech-dependent. From the onset, Michelle could avoid communication by text for a prescribed amount of time. By communicating openly via phone call or in person, she can practice reading the body language and voice intonation of her partner. This will enable both Michelle and the therapist to evaluate the accuracy of her perceptions. Although Michelle had previously considered herself undoubtedly self-secure, this experience really threw her for a loop. I was able to help her see this experience as an opportunity to examine her vulnerabilities, which was ultimately a catalyst for positive growth.

THERAPY OR NOT: FOR THE GHOSTER

Due to the nature of ghosting behavior, ghosters usually do not get direct feedback from the person hurt by their actions. Because they are often unaware of the extent of the anger and mistrust they caused, they can more easily avoid their own feelings. Surely the research is underreported, as people do not necessarily admit to their ghosting behaviors. My hypothesis is that although it is easier to inadequately terminate text relationships, people who do so may have difficulty in communicating contentious feelings face-to-face, as well.

So, let's say you are a ghoster. If you admit it and feel ashamed, you are ahead of the game. Feeling guilty for your actions motivates you to be proactive and modify your behavior. What can you do about it? You can search for the elusive G.A. meeting (Ghosters Anonymous), although I am not sure it exists. More realistically, therapy can be helpful in working through your ghosting habit.

The first question is, why are you ghosting? Does it come from fear of confrontation, shame, or guilt? Are you, like the person I interviewed, someone who tends to avoid conflict? In essence, do you feel like you are saving the other person from feeling rejected? If you do ghost, this avoidant behavior probably manifests itself differently in face-to-face relationships. Developing insight into the behavior would unequivocally have a positive impact on the quality of your relationships.

The ghoster I interviewed responded well to my challenge to put himself in the place of the other. One ghoster explained in a *Huffington Post* article, "Even after one or two dates [the people you meet online] are still a profile to you, not a person. I don't feel the normal empathy I would for someone I met organically."[6] Perhaps using dating apps creates a false reality that the other person is more of an illusion than a real person. The texting phase may preclude sensitivity because of the limited information shared through this format. If you are on a dating app and this is your experience, try to elicit a more substantial conversation.

Utilizing a cognitive behavioral approach could be helpful if you ghosted in the past. This requires making the behavioral change first and seeing if your thoughts and feelings transform in response. Start calling rather than texting. Ask your partner out sooner than later to discover if there is a connection. If there is not, chances are good the other person feels similarly and it can be a mutually agreed upon, quick, and painless termination.

If the reason you ghost is that you do not know what to say and prefer to avoid conflict, try practicing with someone safe (i.e., a therapist) or someone else nonjudgmental. It is hard to get the feeling right in the written word. If you feel a need to end a texting relationship, write out some phrases first and read them to yourself and/or others. Undoubtedly, they will feel harsh, but in the long run, the fact that you tried to communicate would probably be appreciated.

If you find yourself inordinately struggling to end a text relationship, more than likely this is also reflected in all of your interpersonal relationships.

The same strategy would apply. Try out a few phrases in therapy or with a friend to see how they sound. Developing a toolbox of words that you can pull from, if necessary, could reduce your anxiety and eventually enable you to communicate your feelings more naturally.

If these methodologies do not work for you, you can try a slow detox to wean off the behavior. In this case, you can try what *Vogue* termed as the "soft ghost."[7] Soft ghost is when you fade out in steps. The goal would be to resolve a specific situation, but in the end, work toward changing your behavior. To do this, you would first wait before texting back in order to construct an appropriate short response. After a few days, once you have reflected on why you want the relationship to end, you can give your partner a call, take responsibility for your short responses, and verbalize the reason for detaching. This is perhaps not an ideal way to dissolve a relationship. However, it gives both parties time to process what is going on and provides the opportunity for clear communication in the end.

In one of the focus groups I conducted, a woman in her 20s discussed how she used to ghost others until she experienced a heartbreaking ghosting herself. She was able to take a second look at the way she treated others and decided that she would never ghost again. Instead, she crafted a reusable template to text to the guys she connected to on the dating app. She shared with me the clever text template that reads as follows: "Hey, had a great time. I'm afraid I'm feeling more of a friend vibe. Nothing against you, you're a great guy, just want to be honest and not lead you on." Samantha has received great feedback from guys in response to this text, who have thanked her for being honest. Regardless of whether she received a text back, she felt guiltless and satisfied. Samantha explained that when she was ghosted, she spent a week overanalyzing until she finally concluded that her partner clearly had issues with communication. If he could not be straight and honest with her during that stage of the relationship, she probably was better off moving on altogether. She made a good point in that communication is key in relationships. Ultimately, you cannot just disappear or "flu powder away" (for those Harry Potter fans) anytime you are upset, anxious, or insecure. So if you get ghosted, remind yourself that you are ultimately better off finding someone with the ability to directly communicate his or her thoughts and feelings.

CASE STUDY: CUSHIONING

Sarah, 24, was just learning and appreciating dating apps when she met Linda, 26, at a bar. They had an instant connection and went on a couple of dates. They certainly had a great sexual chemistry, and Sarah was starting to really like Linda. However, Sarah was worried about becoming too invested in a relationship when she had only just entered the world of dating apps. She was also afraid of becoming too vulnerable with Linda and losing control in the relationship. Therefore, she continued to date Linda while also exploring other relationships through the dating apps. She chatted with other people consistently and occasionally met up with them for dates. Sarah's main focus was on Linda, but if the relationship went sour, she had "cushions to soften the fall." In this case, Sarah's intense passion for Linda caused her to feel anxious and consequently diffuse her energy with other prospects.

ANALYSIS: WHAT IS CUSHIONING?

Ghosting is a behavior that has become more prevalent with the advent of dating apps. This chapter should have given you a better sense of why it happens, along with either techniques to cope as the ghostee and strategies to change (if you desire) as the ghoster. Recently, the term "cushioning" has emerged as another facet of online dating. Again, this is historically similar to the dating experience but amplified due to modern technology. Just like ghosting, exploring the reasons behind cushioning can illuminate one's fears and goals in regard to dating.

RESEARCH: CUSHIONING

According to Roisin Lanigan, " 'Cushioning' means while you are still having your main thing, you keep a few others on the backburner, texting them and giving them just enough attention so that if your main relationship goes down, you are not totally left alone."[8] You know how you get anxious or overthink when you are casually dating someone. It is frustrating because you become this insecure person who obsessively scrutinizes the relationship. Sometimes it even messes everything up because you start freaking out over the smallest mishaps. Perhaps you haven't heard from your partner in a day, or you misread one of his or her texts. This quickly turns into nights of not sleeping, loss of appetite, and overall panic. Some people have figured out a way to work through this problematic behavior: cushioning.

According to Bela Gandhi of Today.com, "Cushioning is what we used to call having a backup plan or plan B—basically, someone waiting in the wings. It is having other dating options in case the current relationship fizzles."[9] Basically, once you like someone, you decide you don't want to put all your eggs in one basket. Because, God forbid, if something goes wrong, you'll end up with nothing. So, instead of obsessing about your current relationship and worrying about all future scenarios, you side-text other potential partners. Now, these other potentials aren't *really* in the running. You definitely don't like them as much as your main squeeze. However, they are somewhat entertaining, always respond to your texts, and provide a necessary distraction. You are so scared of somehow either messing up the relationship or getting hurt that you have real, human, backup plans to use as defense mechanisms.

IMPLICATIONS FOR THERAPISTS: DISCUSSING INTENT

Exploring intent in relation to action is helpful in understanding if the cushioning behavior is ego-syntonic (the behavior and intent correlate). Before technology existed, individuals could certainly date multiple partners to decide if they liked one better than another. However, they had to actually put energy and time into each of their potential suitors because they had to meet face-to-face and engage in conversations. The relationships ended when either party deemed it unworthy of the time and/or effort. Technology, on the other hand, makes it easy to continue a relationship with minimal exertion. Individuals can text or message through an app just to engage in conversations while simultaneously dating their primary partner.

Encouraging clients to explore potential outcomes of their relationships can promote self-awareness. Sometimes, side relationships are indicative of a fear of intimacy. In these cases, cushioning provides the catalyst to explore a weakness that would impact the growth of any intimate relationship. I sometimes acknowledge this with clients by letting them know that it is a good thing they acted out in this way as it has allowed us to address this pattern. On the other hand, cushioning could be a sign of narcissism or another result of people forgetting that there is an actual person on the other side of the app. If and when the client becomes aware that cushioning is a direct result of his or her fear of intimacy, then exploring his or her vulnerability would be a good therapeutic goal. If the client's goal is to reduce anxiety by keeping an open mind to other potential partners, then perhaps this behavior is not the worst idea. Ultimately, if clients are mindful as to the reasons for their actions and are consequently in better control of their behaviors, then self-esteem will naturally improve. Acting from a place of insecurity can lead to harmful decisions that create more possibilities to feel anxious.

IMPLICATION FOR THERAPISTS: DISCUSSING OPENNESS AND HONESTY

Using technology to communicate sometimes alleviates the pressure to be totally transparent with a partner. When working with clients who often communicate through text, I find it helpful to encourage them to ask more difficult questions through that channel. For example, someone could ask the person he is dating if she is pursuing other partners. At this point, they can also get a better sense of whether or not they plan to be exclusive. Problems arise when the intentions of both parties are not clear. One person might be engaging in cushioning secretly, while the other person assumes a level of exclusiveness. My advice is not to assume the other's intention especially in the beginning stages of a relationship.

This is where it could be helpful to stress open communication in a therapeutic setting. One question to ask your client is: What are the ground rules of your relationship? Another question might be: Are you aware of the expectations that your partner has for the relationship? If there is a clear understanding by both parties that dating other people is allowed, then there is no harm. Openly discussing the status of the relationship is a way of showing respect to each other. It also sets the stage for a potentially moral ending of a relationship. If your clients are unsure and anxious about their partner's level of exclusiveness, coach them to ask in a casual way to help relieve some of the uncertainty. It can be a daunting conversation, as they are unsure how their partners will respond. However, the alternative is to continue the relationship in angst until their partner initiates the conversation. Role-playing these conversations in therapy can assist in easing some of that fear. If clients feel confident in the language and how they want to broach the topic, then a level of insecurity can be removed.

For both the ghostee and the ghoster, the online experience is often a reflection of issues that occur in face-to-face relationships. It is possible that neither party emerges from the experience feeling pleased or self-confident. Addressing the intentions of both individuals and working toward behavioral changes would have a positive impact on their ultimate social and interpersonal goals. Becoming mindful of their own needs and how their actions affect others can lead clients to a more constructive dating experience.

SUMMARY

Ghosting and cushioning are behaviors that have existed throughout history but have become more prevalent because of dating apps. The ease of meeting a potential match can have many implications that we are just beginning to understand through research studies. Due to the myriad supply of anonymous suitors, there is less pressure to treat anyone as special. The reason one would choose to ghost or cushion can also change over time. Confronting someone that you are uninterested in is awkward and uncomfortable. Alternatively, it is natural to fear putting all your eggs in one basket. Being vulnerable requires strength and a willingness to take risks.

It is possible that you are not utilizing the apps to meet a long-term partner, but are seeking to network, hook up, or casually date. The biggest change is to be mindful about how your actions affect others. People have different reasons for swiping, which are not necessarily shared with the person with whom they match. However, when your realize that you and your partner have alternative goals for the relationship, it is better to reveal your intention sooner rather than later, to avoid leading someone on.

Whether you are a ghostee or a ghoster, exploring the motivations for the behavior will help to improve all your relationships. If you notice a pattern of ghosting or cushioning, try to understand why you repeat the same behaviors. Are you allowing yourself to immerse yourself fully in the relationship? Are you ultimately working to meet your end goal, whether to find a relationship or to date casually? According to Jen Kim, a writer for *Psychology Today*, "Cognitive dissonance is what is also making ghosting more and more commonplace—the more we excuse the behavior, the more we can convince ourselves that it's normal and acceptable."[10] This type of behavior is so normalized that sometimes people do not think twice before ghosting or cushioning. It is commonplace to end a relationship with ghosting, especially at the beginning stages.

In this chapter's opening case study, Michelle experienced rejection and disappointment. She probably would have felt similarly if Greg broke up with her in person. However, the fact that he ghosted her made her feel that she misjudged him. She thought he was the type of person who would take responsibility for his actions and understand she deserved a goodbye. In this case, we do not really know what Greg was perceiving, feeling, or even thinking. Initially, Michelle's description of his personality and behaviors prior to the ghosting did not shed adequate light as to why he so abruptly ended the relationship. At one point, she even became worried, thinking he may have had an accident. However, once Michelle regained her self-assurance, we were able to look more closely at Greg's dating behavior. He tended to become impatient, requiring a response soon after he texted anything. He was less responsive when Michelle texted him. Although this is not a known indicator of a potential ghoster, Michelle realized she did not perceive this as neediness, but in retrospect, she now believes it to be a red flag. If their relationship consisted of fewer texts and more voice contacts, this may have been more evident. It is often easier to respond quickly to a text than to a phone message. In this way, the technology may indeed be exacerbating the phenomena of precipitously ending relationships without closure.

It appears that dating apps may contribute to a reduced sensitivity toward new acquaintances. There is something to be said about looking someone in the eye while you end a relationship. It shows you have a certain level of respect for your partner. As communicating through texts and apps increases in prevalence, society in general may become more adept at "reading through the emojis."

Chapter 11

HOW PARENTS CAN SUPPORT THEIR CHILDREN

If you have read this book completely, you now understand the many ways technology can influence relationships, in both harmful and helpful ways. So, how do we develop the skill sets and values to balance and navigate the world of technology? How do we prevent technology from controlling relationships, decreasing self-esteem, and becoming an addiction?

Just like with any other mind-set or behavior, we develop specific ideas and viewpoints from our upbringing. The lessons you learned from your parents, caretakers, or extended family affect the way you see the world. Certainly, there are ways to create your own path and form your own opinion; however, our core values grow from the messages received during childhood.

With this in mind, I thought it necessary to discuss ways for parents to speak to their children about technology. This chapter also provides tips and tools for creating the essential boundaries to prevent technology from taking control. If you are not a parent/do not plan on becoming a parent, this chapter is still helpful in creating meaningful discussions with family and friends.

I will take you on a journey with parents Melinda and Bill, their son Steven and daughter Sasha, from childhood through the teen years. This family's narrative is a compilation of different presenting problems of diverse families.

CASE STUDY: MELINDA AND BILL AND THEIR YOUNG CHILDREN

Melinda and Bill were overwhelmed with full-time jobs and raising two children. Steven, age 7, was a hyperactive and rambunctious kid. He was social with his peers, and he loved singing and playing sports. Sasha, age 5, had just started kindergarten. She was more introverted than Steven was, and she was having difficulty mingling with the other students. Melinda and Bill had a babysitter watch Steven and Sasha until one of them returned home around 7 p.m.

The school psychologist, Jennifer, met with Sasha, as it was school policy to meet with each kindergartener. She asked Sasha to draw a picture of the family. Sasha quietly drew a picture of her, her brother Steven, and the nanny as one unit separated from her parents. When Jennifer questioned why her parents were in the corner, Sasha responded, "They are working." When asked, Sasha said that when she gets home from school, she plays the "dress up game" on the iPad.

THERAPY: MODELING BEHAVIOR

Jennifer scheduled a meeting with Melinda and Bill. After showing them Sasha's picture and asking for a description of a typical day, they both acknowledged the struggle to work full time and raise young children. They bemoaned the fact that they had limited quality time to spend with their children, since they were career-driven and determined to move up in their respective companies. Both parents identified the quality time they shared with their children: driving them to school in the morning and reading to them before bedtime every night.

Jennifer empathized with their situation and noted she was impressed with how they supported each other in accomplishing their goals. She asked if they knew what Steven and Sasha were learning in class. Bill became red with embarrassment and admitted that typically the babysitter helps with any homework and that their role is mostly facilitating the bedtime routine. It became apparent that they did not know the names of their children's close friends. They were ashamed to admit they were unfamiliar with daily occurrences at school.

Jennifer stressed she was not judging them as parents or questioning their love for Steven and Sasha. Melinda and Bill agreed that it would be helpful to gain some guidance and tools to better support their children. Jennifer praised them for personally driving the kids to school and explored what was discussed in the car rides. Melinda responded, "I typically talk on the phone with work through Bluetooth, while Steven sings to himself and Sasha plays on the iPad. They seem to be happy, so I let them be." Bill agreed that this narrative mirrored his experience.

Jennifer moved on to explore their nighttime routine. Bill seemed excited to answer this question and described in detail the books he read to the kids and the funny voices he used to simulate each character. Melinda also valued the pre-bedtime reading, although she sometimes found herself falling asleep mid-book.

Weekends tended to be more family oriented. Both Bill and Melinda explained how, depending on season and weather, they sometimes went to their second home upstate. On Saturdays, they usually played outside in the park or watched movies. On Sundays, both Melinda and Bill caught up on some work while the kids played with their devices.

At the end of the session, Jennifer thanked them for being so honest and forthcoming about their personal lives. She explained, "This is a crucial time period in development for Steven and Sasha. They are learning skills on how to interact with others, developing self-confidence, and forming moral values. The most important thing is for the two of you to show support, interest, and encouragement." Jennifer again expressed empathy that they both lead stressful, overwhelming, and busy lives. She described a few modifications they could make to their everyday routine to help Sasha and Steven thrive and to strengthen the family experience.

1. The car in the morning would be declared a no-technology zone, applicable to *both* parents and children. By using their phone, parents condone technology use in the car. The ride to school is an invaluable opportunity for parents to actively engage with their children about their day, friendships, and encounters. This should also give space to provide compliments, encourage them, and give advice. Active listening demonstrates to Sasha and Steven that their parents are present and are interested in their lives.

2. Reading to the children is meaningful but does not replace face-to-face, interactive conversation. Jennifer suggested scheduling one midweek family dinner designated as a technology-free discussion about their kids' lives and friendships. Small periods of quality time together would enrich their relationships and set a foundation for ongoing communication, even though their time is limited. Nights they are unable to make it home on time, they should attempt to connect during the bedtime reading period. Prior to reading stories, they should ask questions about the children's day, about homework assignments, and about anything else that happened in the classroom. Compliments and words of encouragement are helpful. The children will feel more confident when going to sleep, which will give them a more peaceful rest and a better start to their day.

3. Jennifer validated the value of the family's outdoor time. They enjoyed participating in outdoor activities together, and the children were physically healthy. Jennifer described the risk of childhood obesity for children who spend too much time indoors with devices. She encouraged them to schedule playdates for their children to promote socialization, which in turn could lead to friendships for themselves with other parents.

Jennifer reemphasized the importance of having quality time without technology. When Melinda and Bill utilize their phones or computer, they are suggesting they are busy, distracted, and uninterested. The children can potentially feel sidelined when parents direct their energy toward their devices.

Steven and Sasha observed their parents engaging with technology and minimally socializing with others. This behavior set an example prioritizing technology over friendships. Using the iPad sparingly can be helpful when playing educational games. However, there needs to be an appropriate balance. Additionally, Melinda and Bill would model the values of friendship, family, and health by limiting their own use of technology.

CASE STUDY: MELINDA AND BILL DURING THEIR CHILDREN'S TEENAGE YEARS

Steven, now 15 years old, was having difficulty focusing in school. His teachers were concerned because he seemed tired. They knew his potential and were worried about his inability to concentrate. The school psychologist, James, spoke to Steven and told him that his teachers had been noticing a change in his ability to focus and stay awake throughout the day. James asked him about life at home and about his bedtime routine. Steven responded that life at home was fine and that he got into bed around 10 p.m. James enquired about what he does when he gets into bed, and Steven responded that he scrolls through social media, sports news, or texts his friends. Steven described his inability to fall asleep and his tendency to wake up throughout the night. James quickly identified the source of Steven's insomnia and sleep disturbance, which directly affected his schoolwork and energy level.

Sasha, 13 years old, was now in seventh grade and was navigating the world of cliques, bullies, and social media. Her parents purchased her a cell phone to call them when she got home from school and to fit in with her friends who texted in a group thread. Although Bill and Melinda were skeptical about whether Sasha was old enough, they ultimately wanted her to be happy.

However, recently they noticed that Sasha was acting withdrawn. When they got home at night and asked her about the day, she seemed quieter than usual. When they asked her what was wrong, she simply shrugged and said, "I'm fine."

THERAPY: SETTING BOUNDARIES

Bill and Melinda were brought into school to discuss Steven's insomnia. James said that Steven could try melatonin as a sleep aid, but more importantly, he would have to change his behavior in regard to his cell phone use. James explained that the light from the phone could have an impact on Steven's sleep cycle. The blinking light from the phone could disrupt his sleep. Additionally, the material he was viewing could create anxiety, which subsequently leads to insomnia.

James explained, "I know it's hard to part from our phones sometimes. Even I keep my phone on my nightstand. However, for health reasons, it is really better to keep our phones off, in a different room, while we sleep. Creating boundaries is helpful, not only for our kids, but for us, as well!"

Bill and Melinda agreed to talk to Steven about modifying his behavior, as well as their own. They decided to buy an alarm clock after the session so they wouldn't have to rely on their phones. When they finished discussing Steven, they shared their concerns about Sasha.

They described Sasha as acting withdrawn, avoiding questions, and spending a lot of time in her room. This troubled them, and they sought guidance, even though they realized that some might describe this as typical teenage behavior. James told them it was a good idea to continue asking her questions, regardless of whether she chose to disclose. James provided some general advice and mentioned that he would speak to the middle-school psychologist.

James also offered additional advice:

> Try asking questions not related to her behavior. Don't ask general questions like, "What's wrong?" or "How was your day?" Or "Why are you quiet?" Instead, try asking, "What's going on with _____ (insert one of her friends' name)?" Ask her what social media she uses. The key is to be involved but not intrusive. If you get a better sense of the specifics in her life, then perhaps it will clue you into what is wrong. Therapy will also be helpful because it is possible that Sasha is embarrassed and she may be more likely to share with an unbiased professional.

Bill and Melinda agreed to call the school psychologist and try asking more open-ended questions regarding Sasha's friends and social media preferences. They wondered aloud if they should take her phone to locate any material that may be causing the anxiety. James advised them to take it one step at a time. It is important that Sasha also feel respected. Taking and snooping through her phone is an invasion of her privacy. Before crossing that line, they should try other means to determine the cause of her behavior.

James left them with one more piece of advice:

> No matter what, don't get angry. This can be a tough time for adolescents. There could be bullying, peer pressure, or just feeling left out. This is not so different from what we experienced when we were younger. The only addition is that technology exacerbates those feelings and creates additional forms of anxiety. So be patient, understanding, and just show your support.

CASE STUDY: BILL AND MELINDA'S TEENAGE DRIVERS

As Steve approached 17 years of age and became a young driver, both modeling and limit setting became pivotal. No parent should text and drive or use anything other than a "hands-free" device. This rule should be followed at all times, not just when a child is in the car, because invariably children will hear about or observe their parent "doing it." Rules for phone use and driving need to be clear with enforceable repercussions. In this regard, parents should be in cahoots with other parents, reporting if any of their children are seen being distracted by technology when driving. If parents are on the same page, it is more likely their children will follow the behavior.

CASE STUDY: HELICOPTER PARENTS—PREPARING FOR STEVEN AND SASHA'S COLLEGE EXPERIENCE

In the past, communication from afar was limited. College students rarely had a landline they could use to call long distance. Long-distance phone conversations were expensive, and therefore they were planned and intermittent. Now, there is a need for instant gratification and a quick reply. Parents, accustomed to easily reaching their children, become worried when they are inaccessible. World terror events have reinforced this, as the need for immediate connection becomes a real factor in acknowledging safety. However, despite this invaluable tool, adolescents still need the opportunity to individuate. College-age young adults require space to make mistakes and to grow.

Parents can discuss with their children ways to communicate that respect their boundaries. Perhaps college students can update their parents through text and make a point to call occasionally to check in. Parents need to be understanding and flexible. Instead of leaving an abundance of voicemails (that the kids do not listen to) hoping to get a return call, they can text and say they are just checking in and hope everything is going well.

A mobile phone is an indispensable tool in assuring safety, especially for college students. There are particular apps to support students, especially those away from home for the first time, many of which can lead to meaningful and important discussions. For example, if children are driving to school, discussing texting and driving is an important message and topic. Apps such as Find My iPhone, CampusSafe, and Circle of 6 are especially beneficial for college students. Find my iPhone utilizes a GPS to track a lost or stolen phone. However, young adults need to know to exercise good judgment and not try to recover a stolen phone without the authorities. CampusSafe, founded by University of Rochester Institute of Technology Students, sets up a one-touch dial of campus police and other emergency, healthcare, and counseling numbers. Users are able to directly text campus police to report minor incidents. A critical feature is the emergency button, which, when pushed, notifies campus police of the student's identity and GPS location, and begins immediate communication. Circle of 6 enables a user to choose six emergency contacts. These contacts are sent a prewritten text message that clandestinely alerts them that the user is in trouble and requires immediate assistance. A GPS location and map are transmitted with the option to notify 9-1-1 or a sex abuse hotline instantaneously.

Sasha and Steven have unique personalities, and, like most college students, they will encounter personal and social challenges. Bill and Melinda can feel assured that they promoted their children's confidence. Sasha and Steven know they have their parents' trust. All family members are aware of the importance of being respectful of each other's space yet staying connected. Sasha and Steven also know they have their parents' full support if they need additional assistance or guidance.

RESEARCH: GIVE ME THE NUMBERS

Researchers have observed and studied the impact technology has had on adults and children. However, it is essential to create techniques and educate parents now that the implications of technology use have been identified. The following are statistics reported from Common Sense Media, based on surveys from more than 1,700 parents of children ages 8 to 18.[1] Participants described their own media use as well as perceptions of how their children engaged with media and technology.

1. Parents with tweens and teens spend more than nine hours a day with screen media, with 82 percent of that time devoted to personal screen media.

2. Fifty percent of parents indicated they thought using social media hurts children's physical activity.

3. Fewer parents in the study believed social media had negative consequences on children's ability to focus (35%), face-to-face communication (34%), behavior (24%), school performance (22%), emotional well-being (20%), or relationships with friends (15%).

4. Over half (56%) of all parents indicated concern that their children may become addicted to technology.

5. Parents of tweens (57%) were more likely than parents of teens (27%) to check their children's devices and social media accounts "always" or "most of the time."

6. A majority of parents reported mobile devices are not allowed during family meals (78%) or during bedtime (63%).

7. Most parents (68%) reported their children are allowed to use mobile devices in the car when they are passengers.

These statistics describe a society consumed with devices. For the first time, we are observing a group of young parents who were exposed to technology prior to adulthood. Toddlers are interacting with iPads before they can verbalize sentences, and young children have become adept at working an iPhone before riding a bicycle. It is amazing to watch them teach themselves how to swipe and open a phone before walking.

Parents are becoming increasingly aware of the epidemic of childhood obesity; however, their own lifestyles do not sufficiently emphasize physical activity. They encourage their children to run around outside, while they sit on the sidelines with their face in their phones. Take a trip to the playground and

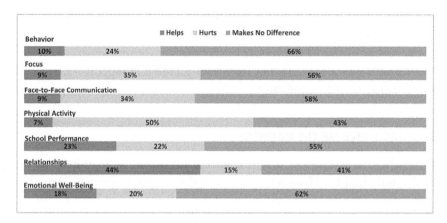

Figure 11.1 Parents Who Believe Their Children's Use of Social Media Helps, Hurts, or Makes No Difference, by Child Outcome. (Lauricella, A. R., Cingel, D. P., Beaudoin-Ryan, L., Robb, M. B., Saphir, M., & Wartella, E. A. (2016). *The Common Sense Census: Plugged-In Parents of Tweens and Teens.* San Francisco, CA: Common Sense Media. Used by permission of Common Sense Media)

observe. Watch the kids run around, while the parents or sitters text on the benches. Not only is this sedentary lifestyle harmful for the parents' health, but it is also a missed opportunity to interact, engage, and bond with their kids.

At this point, less is known about the long-term effects of technology use on academic success, concentration, learning styles, social skills, and emotional well-being. Even though this impact might be difficult to quantify, there is an immediate need for teachers to adjust their curriculums to address decreasing attention spans. Parental underestimation of the influence of technology on academic learning (as outlined earlier) could have very harmful consequences because they may fail to demand the changes in the classroom that their children need.

RESEARCH: WHAT'S THE DAMAGE?

If you are not a numbers person, then maybe the following information will be clearer in terms of the detrimental impact of technology. Dr. Mari Swingle is a clinical psychologist and practicing clinician. Her postdoctoral work described the effects of technology on brain function. She found that all of us "are functioning in significantly higher states of arousal. Accordingly, the rates of anxious depression, anxiety, and insomnia are skyrocketing, as can be seen in pharmaceutical sales and rates of prevalence in the general population."[2] Even young children are experiencing higher states of arousal in their brains, which is making it harder to find an "off switch." This arousal can cause slower functional attention and higher anxiety. Additionally, feeling constantly "revved" can lead to fatigue, irritability, and depression. She calls this "techno-brain burnout."

Dr. Swingle also tackles the effects that societal and familial expectations are having on children. The expectations to perform in school, take college-level courses at an early age, or excel at an activity are at a new level. According to Dr. Swingle, "We have grown accustomed to, and now want, expect, even demand, reward for mere participation rather than proof of excellence."[3] She feels tech gaming indeed does reward for mere participation in that the games are created to stimulate reinforcement at the perfect rate. That is one reason why games like Candy Crush are so addictive. In Candy Crush, the players are faced with the opportunity to move to the next level as a reward for reaching a certain objective. When they advance, they feel stimulated by the gratification of success. This motivates them to continue playing, until they receive the next reward.

Dr. Swingle found that children prefer Internet-based games to other activities due to the immediate reward and satisfying feeling gained from the interaction. In general, if we mess up in sports, music, or art, we either quit or need an external motivating force to continue. Many children are not bothering to train or to "mess up" and prefer the immediate gratification and amusement of gaming. She also argues for an appropriate balance, which means parents need to take a stance on the types of activities in which their children are involved.

SO WHAT NOW?

The first step in creating change is accepting that technology is present and that moderation is key. NPR featured an online tool developed by the American Academy of Pediatrics, which is designed to help parents create their own family media plan.[4] It is an interactive experience that lets parents set guidelines for each child. They also provide age-specific recommendations and space to accommodate your own specific rules. Once the plan is created, you can print it out and have your own family media policy page.

The process takes about five minutes. You can indicate the technology-free zones in the household, times of day when technology is restricted, how and when you will watch media with your children, and what media you will avoid. When you do allow yourselves to engage with technology, you should partake in "co-viewing" with your children. Georgene Troseth, associate professor of psychology at Vanderbilt University, says that watching or using media with your child should mimic reading a book together.[5] You should talk to them about what you're watching and compare it to the real world. According to Troseth, "That's a valuable skill to work on, since that's how adults use media: we use it to get information or to be entertained." Ultimately, the family's media guidelines should be formed with their personal values in mind, as well as what the science indicates are healthy behaviors.

The American Academy of Pediatrics makes it clear that the plan is not going to automatically solve the issues or change the behaviors. However, it creates clear and concise guidelines that are openly laid out and to which parents can refer when needed. The doctors agree children should not sleep with their devices in their room and should avoid exposure for one hour before bedtime. Additionally, they need to balance indoor playtime with outdoor physical activity. Informing children about online safety, bullying, and appropriate use of social media becomes an ongoing conversation as children's exposure and network expand.

Starting from an early age, parents have a huge role in implementing rules and instilling values. This can help inform how children respond to issues related to technology later in life. Keeping up with the continual changes can be arduous. However, parents need to be acquainted with the technology so they can guide and provide reasonable limits for their children.

Lastly, parents should observe and react accordingly to their child's behavior. Trusting your gut and asking for help is the best practice in determining the best treatment strategy. Children often like being on the teaching end, so parents could take advantage of this dynamic and have their children explain the technology. Especially when they are young, it is exciting for them to feel knowledgeable and to have the opportunity to educate their parents. This also leads to an exploration of the many ways technology can be used to cause both benefit and harm.

TOOLS AND TIPS

I interviewed psychiatrist Dr. Almas Nazir regarding her experience with children and families and their use of media and technology (personal communication). Dr. Nazir emphasized that technology can be helpful for children. Through social media and other channels, they can interact and socialize with peers. It provides children with the opportunity to connect without relying on parent transportation to a play date. There are educational applications, many of which are designed to specifically address the unique learning needs of children with attention deficit disorder and attention-deficit hyperactivity disorder. Preschoolers are learning to read on tablets and are developing reading-readiness skills, facilitating a transition to formal education. The ability to connect remotely with grandparents and other family members becomes an invaluable tool to expand the familial network of families that are separated by distance.

However, she has also seen a rise of anxiety, low self-esteem, and isolation among her young clients. When children are utilizing their devices, they are unable to be present and are shutting themselves out from the world around them. This makes it more difficult to engage in face-to-face interactions and social situations.

Dr. Nazir has also found an increased need for instant gratification, which demonstrates that children's brains are being re-wired. This parallels Dr. Swingle's findings. Children appear to have less ability to maintain concentration than they did in previous generations. They have difficulty focusing, especially on topics that are not as distinctively stimulating. They are lacking the skill set required to pay attention to tasks that are not immediately engaging. Dr. Nazir suggests children should be given a limited amount of time for play and focus on devices. They also need the time to actively engage and learn through other modalities.

If clear rules and boundaries are established from a young age, children will develop the necessary social skills to observe and interpret nonverbal cues from their peers. These particular skills take practice and experience not provided through technology. This will enable them to develop into adults who can react to uncomfortable situations and think on their feet. Scheduling playdates with friends creates opportunities for them to feel included. Encourage games that do not involve technology and instead encourage physical movement.

Dr. Nazir is also seeing a rise in depression and anxiety in young teens and tweens. She finds these conditions more prevalent in females than males, due to the need to fit in with peers on appearance. Social media is influencing this trend by inducing low self-esteem and feelings of rejection and isolation when not included. In addition, social media posts tend to exaggerate the positive and do not present a realistic picture of the lives of others. Especially during childhood and adolescence, differentiating what is seen on social media from the real-life experiences of a peer is challenging. Making up pretend posts with children is a fun way to caution them from believing all that they see. Parents need to educate early on and instill appropriate values. She urges that this type of education is a process and will depend on specific children and situations. However, if the proper foundation is provided early on, and the children have confidence and support, they will be able to thrive, regardless of what comes their way.

Part of education should include having your children imagine themselves in the shoes of others. This will help reinforce inclusion and condemn bullying. If the message is received and reinforced, it will help them better navigate the media world once they begin using phones and computers.

Once children receive cell phones, be mindful and alert of their behaviors. Providing children with a cell phone could be a demonstration of trust and maturity. It could empower them to take more responsibility. For example, texting you when they get home from school, even if there is a babysitter, is one way they could learn to value communication. If you are too strict, it can cause alienation, but remember your job as a parent is not always to make your kid happy.

Encouraging extracurricular activities will help children develop the other side of their brain. They can be creative and use their imaginations. If they become involved in other activities early on, it can help them balance their time spent on devices. Simultaneously, it will help prevent tech addiction or obsession.

Dr. Nazir highly encourages leaving your phone in another room while you sleep. She has found, on both a personal and professional level, a decrease in anxiety and sleep disturbance with the removal of technology during bedtime. She sees clients aged 10, 11, and 12 with insomnia that affects concentration in school and causes decreased energy. Children are scrolling through social media in their beds and are viewing images that are provoking anxiety. They feel left out when they see images of friends and they are excluded. Perhaps because they are also overtired, they may be more susceptible to feeling hurt unnecessarily. It also wires their brains to accelerate, which prevents them from falling asleep.[6]

SUMMARY

Bill and Melinda are typical of modern-day parents who must discover new techniques to deal with the challenges of childrearing presented by constantly evolving technology. It is difficult to preconceive the types of issues your children will face. It is also complicated to assess the impact of technology on a child's social or learning problem. Some parents struggle with an inability to unplug, or they self-criticize their own use of technology, making it even more difficult to understand the effect on their child. For example, parents who are on their phone at dinnertime may not realize their children miss out on important interactions. They also do not notice that their children are inappropriately using their phones or other devices, as they themselves are distracted and therefore modeling the behavior.

The statistics demonstrate that both parents and children need to modify how they incorporate technology into their lives. At each stage of development, children will need to be guided as they expand their awareness and use of media. Being mindful as to when technology is being used as an escape from socialization versus a tool to enrich one's interaction with the world is not always simple. However, they will take with them the values modeled by their parents.

Setting aside time to speak to your children in a technology-free zone can be extremely healthy and rewarding. As parents, you will certainly discover more insight into their lives. They will feel more cared for and listened to. These are moments that children remember. When children receive adequate attention in the home, they will thrive. They will also further develop the necessary interpersonal skills to socialize in a school setting (without the use of technology). Lastly, spending time outside and encouraging participation in extracurricular activities can increase their health, positivity, and social group.

We are just beginning to understand the effects of technology on our brain wiring. Children are starting to grow up on iPads and are receiving phones at earlier ages. We need to recognize the role that technology plays as a modality to support children's education. In many cases, it has been an incredibly valuable tool for children who have learning, social, and emotional issues. It is unclear what long-term effects this will have on cognitive development. What is clear from the research and the specialists is that moderation is key. Open communication, showing support, and building confidence are the best techniques to help your children learn moderation and thrive as they mature and develop.

Chapter 12

FINAL THOUGHTS, TIPS, AND STRATEGIES

Technology is all around us and is impossible to avoid. Once we accept that fact, increasing our awareness of its function and determining its proper place in our lives enables us to maintain control. When we are in mindful control of technology (instead of mindlessly allowing it to control us), we can address the obstacles it presents and manipulate it in ways that support our relationships. Our conscious use of technology can actually lead to increased connection and closeness.

You have now read numerous case studies and narratives that explore the many issues related to how technology affects our daily lives. In each chapter, you were given techniques and methods that can guide you on a more mindful and self-reflective journey toward a healthy and balanced use of technology in your life and relationships. Take a moment and think about your own relationships, whether romantic, familial, or social. How much energy are you currently dedicating to those relationships? How much do you know about these individuals, their lives, their stressors, their goals, their dreams, and their fears? Seriously, put down the book (and/or your phone) and take a minute.

Now think about how much time you dedicate to social media, swiping, scrolling, watching, and playing on your devices. Is there room to shift the focus away from your screens and redirect some of that energy back toward your relationships, strengthening and enhancing those bonds? One small change can make a world of difference, not only for your relationships, but for your mental health, as well. You know how distracting technology can be and how easily you can get lost in the alternate reality of social media. However, if you spend more energy in the here and now, with the people around you, you will build and foster your IRL ("in real life") interpersonal connections.

People often use their phone, play Internet games, or swipe on dating apps to avoid confronting internal or interpersonal issues. Sometimes a person who is trying to ignore the reality that he or she is not getting what he or she needs from a relationship will use the distraction provided by technology as a coping method. The unique quality of every relationship means there is not one solution or treatment. The aim of this book is to educate you about the range of issues that individuals experience in regard to technology and dating. I hope that you are able to take at least one lesson away and create a realistic goal for yourself to improve your use of devices.

It is certainly not easy to change a behavior, so I want you to also be easy on yourself and your partner (current or future). Discussing these topics with friends or partners is the first step in transformation. Disclose your vulnerability, explore why you decide to use your device, and embrace the freedom you feel when you step away from technology. If you are in a relationship, it can be fun to practice this as a team. Challenge yourselves to go on airplane mode (meaning you're not connected to the Internet via any devices) a couple nights a week and focus on each other. Not only will this be a gift for your mind, but also a chance to nurture intimacy.

On the other hand, you also read about a few couples who successfully utilized technology to enhance their relationships and love lives. The tech products currently being produced to increase intimacy, whether in person or long distance, are sincerely mind-blowing (I still cannot even fathom that Bluetooth can control a vibrator from a different state). Interviewing experts in the field and founders of companies for this book was extremely rewarding. I want to express my utmost regard for those founders in paving the way for sexologists and researchers alike.

It is often difficult to communicate with a partner the desire to experiment with toys. Many times, individuals feel they are inadequate if toys are necessary to climax. Try approaching the conversation from a different direction. Instead of suggesting there is anything wrong, explain to your partner that you are looking to enhance the intimacy in your relationship. After all, there is always room for improvement. Discuss if tech-based sex toys are something that either of you want to explore. Be open-minded to hearing the fantasies of your partner but also be sure to voice hesitancies. That way, both parties begin with an understanding of the other's needs, which makes it safe to consent to experiment.

Technology should be thought of as a tool in your toolbox. Before picking up a hammer or a screwdriver, you first assess the situation at hand. Are you hanging up a picture with nails? Do you require a screw to attach your drawer to your dresser? Regardless of the task at hand, you are mindful of the instrument you need before rummaging around the toolbox. The same thought process could be employed with technology. What are you looking to do right now? Do you want to take the night off to unwind, relax, and zone out? If so, which devices are necessary at this time? Perhaps you want to watch a random show on television. If this is the case, then is your phone essential?

If you need to dedicate additional time for work when you leave the office, think to yourself which devices are required. Perhaps only your computer, which has your e-mail and work software on it, is needed to get the job done. In that case, remove your phone and keep the television off to focus on your task. Not only is this a mindfulness exercise, but work productivity will certainly increase as well. If productivity increases, then the time you can spend on family, friends, and a significant other can be more meaningful, as well.

As advances in technology bring us closer and closer to an existence based on artificial reality, we must constantly be asking ourselves how we can ensure that technology serves only to enhance our lives. We must guard against *becoming* technology.

I know I threw a lot of tools and tips at you throughout the book. I also know, from personal experience, how hard it can sometimes be to put those techniques into practice. Certainly, it is easier said than done. However, I want to emphasize that it is not about succeeding. The goal is to make small adjustments and to become more conscious and deliberate about how you integrate technology into your life and relationships. Being willing to try, to become more mindful, and to experiment will lead to healthier relationships. And that is what success ultimately looks like. Good luck and enjoy the journey.

ADDENDUM: LESSON PLAN

The issue of technology and relationships should not only be addressed once individuals have started dating. It would be more beneficial to discuss mindfulness in relation to technology use in an educational setting. I mentioned in an earlier chapter that parents should help educate their children about how to value face-to-face interactions and communication. Teachers can also play a role in informing students about the implications of technology use.

A few schools are beginning to offer classes related to the impact of technology on relationships. George Washington University in Washington, D.C., offers a class titled "Sex and Tech," taught by Dr. Susan Milstein, which explores how technology plays a role in relationships and affects intimacy. I have created a lesson plan that can be utilized in both high schools and universities, which encourages students to reflect on their own use of technology, while discussing as a class the implications it has for relationships.

A class on this specific topic provides students with the opportunity to be more mindful of their own behavior and to create positive changes in their everyday lives. They can learn from each other and engage in meaningful discussions about why it is so difficult to be removed from technology.

The feedback I received after implementing this lesson was incredible. Students were appreciative of the opportunity to share how this phenomenon affects the quality of their life. They recognized the benefits of being more conscious of how and when they were using technology. As universities and high schools begin to incorporate this into their curriculum, more students will grow personally and professionally by becoming more cognizant adults.

LESSON TITLE: DATING, RELATING, AND INNOVATING: THE DISTRACTIONS OF TECHNOLOGY

Lesson topic: How Technology Can Be Distracting in Both Romantic Relationships and Friendships

> Time: One hour
> Audience: 30 students in a college class, mixture of Freshman, Sophomores, Juniors and Seniors

Rationale: The use of technology affects levels of intimacy and the ability to form emotional bonds. Eighty-nine percent of respondents of a 2015 Pew Research Study said they had used their phone during their most recent social gathering, most often to read a text or e-mail, take a photo, or send a text.[1] Sherry Turkle, the author of *Alone Together: Why We Expect More from Technology and Less from Each Other*,[2] says, "We've gotten used to being connected all the time, but we have found ways around conversation—at least from conversation that is open-ended and spontaneous, in which we play with ideas and allow ourselves to be fully present and vulnerable."[3]

It is not a coincidence that phone addiction is becoming a mainstream debate in the media and mental health associations.[4] The presence of the phone and computer draws a couples' attention and energy away from each other and toward their devices. As a result, intimacy decreases and individuals find themselves emotionally and physically distanced. It is becoming increasingly difficult to detach from social media, professional/school expectations, and external stressors. The need to connect and be available through technology is common and detrimental to relationships.

Students in college who attend this seminar will have the ability to process and discuss the impact of technology on both romantic relationships and friendships. As a result of the lesson, students will practice increased mindfulness and self-awareness, and will be able to implement behavioral changes. They will be able to reduce the technological distractions they experience and will notice improvements in relationships.

Lesson goal: Students will understand how technology is distracting in friendships and in romantic relationships.

Lesson objectives: *Focus on increasing students' knowledge around technological distractions on intimate relationships and identify areas of personal application:*

1. Students will identify six ways that technology can be distracting.

2. Students will discover and discuss how they utilize technology.

3. Students will apply tools given to modify their own technological distractions.

Materials Needed: Projector and computer for PowerPoint presentation, index cards (any size is OK)

Preparation:

Write six scenarios (examples below) on index cards

Write seven poll questions on PollAnywhere.Com

Download Poll Anywhere Chrome Extension so that Poll Anywhere questions can be placed in Google Slides. Search YouTube for video instructions, if necessary.

Buy several plastic phones for role playing purposes.

Create PowerPoint presentation that:

- Includes Poll Anywhere questions.
- Includes process questions for scenes.
- Ends with tools and tips for students.

Arrange classroom chairs in groups of five.

Lesson outline:

1. **Introduction (3 minutes):** Introduce self and professional background. It is important that students understand and appreciate the reason the course was constructed. Additionally, stress the rule that cell phones and laptops are to be put away in bag prior to class beginning, unless *otherwise instructed by professor.* This coincides with mission of class and specifically this lecture.

2. **(3 minutes)** Introduce facts and statistics from Pew Research Study.[5] Examples:

   - 82% of respondents say that using a phone in social settings hurts conversations
   - 88% of respondents believe it's "generally" not OK to use a cell phone during dinner
   - 89% of respondents said they had used their phone during their most recent social gathering, most often to read a text or e-mail, take a photo, or send a text.

3. **(5 minutes)** Process Stats: What does this mean in terms of use of technology? Is it conscious, deliberate, consistent with student experiences? This is a discussion among the class.

4. **(10 minutes)** Poll Anywhere: Ask questions that will spark debate, conversation, and give perspective on the use of technology. Poll Anywhere is a great source as it is anonymous, so mentioning that before the activity continues is imperative in receiving honest responses. Can be creative with questions and can adapt based on class background and knowledge. Students will be allowed to take out their phones for this exercise but, immediately upon finishing, they will be asked to return them to their bags. Examples:

- Have you been upset or frustrated with a partner being on a phone when you're together?
- Do you use your phone while on the toilet?
- How many times do you look at your phone a day?
- Do you believe in phone addiction?

Move on to next activity after mentioning that the objective of the Poll Anywhere was to just be mindful of use of technology. (Ask students to quickly put away their devices.)

5. **(10 minutes)** Hand out scenario index cards to each group and have the groups plan out roles and scenes. Teacher should hand out fake plastic phones for the scenes so that there is a true neutralization to the learning experience by having none of the participants use their phones. Examples:

   - A couple is out to dinner. One partner is texting, and the other partner is talking on the phone. One person is playing a waiter trying to take their order. Two people are sitting at a nearby table watching the scene unfold. They are getting frustrated because they want the waiter's attention.

   - Three friends are hanging out in the food court watching a YouTube video (your group can decide which one). Meanwhile, a fourth friend is having an altercation with a partner. The friend ends up upset and crying. He or she goes to the food court to vent to his or her friends. Although the friends are empathetic, they can't stop watching the video.

6. **(15 minutes)** Groups act out scenes to each other. (It should be mentioned that there is no discussion in-between scenes, only after all the groups have gone.)

7. **(10 minutes)** Process observations of scenes:

   - Students may observe feelings of anger and/or frustration.
   - Relate to the scenes based on their own experiences.
   - Describe similar situations.
   - Through humor, feel more comfortable identifying aspects of their own behaviors.

8. **Wrap up/tools and tips (7 minutes):** Explain techniques to be more mindful of use of technology and to make behavioral changes:

   - Active listening
   - Openness and honesty
   - Self-awareness—through Virtual-Addiction.Com
   - Mindfulness
   - Accepting feedback
   - Behavioral therapy

Summary: This lesson plan was developed for a college-level course but can be modified for use in a high school environment. Introducing this material at a high school level can help prepare students for the demanding, conflicting pressures of academics and social life in college. Once students leave home, external stressors can often become even more overwhelming than students have previously experienced. If students learn to modify their behavior and to be responsible in their use of technology at an earlier age, they will be better equipped to handle the countless distractions of college. Apps dedicated to budgeting time and geared toward meditation and relaxation may be beneficial in increasing academic performance. In implementing a technology lesson plan for high school students, it would be useful to incorporate these commendable apps (Headspace, RescueTime, Mind42, etc.). *

---

* Please see the endnotes at the end of this book for the sources referenced in this lesson plan.

NOTES

CHAPTER 1

1. Aziz Ansari and Eric Klinenberg, *Modern Romance* (New York: Penguin Press, 2016).

2. Aaron Smith, "Record Shares of Americans Now Own Smartphones, Have Home Broadband," Pew Research Center, January 12, 2017, http://www.pewresearch.org/fact-tank/2017/01/12/evolution-of-technology/.

3. Aaron Smith and Monica Anderson, "5 Facts about Online Dating," Pew Research Center, February 29, 2016, http://www.pewresearch.org/fact-tank/2016/02/29/5-facts-about-online-dating/.

4. Amanda Lenhart, Monica Anderson, and Aaron Smith, "Teens, Technology and Romantic Relationships," Pew Research Center, October 1, 2015, http://www.pewinternet.org/2015/10/01/teens-technology-and-romantic-relationships/.

5. Katherine M. Hertlein, "The Integration of Technology into Sex Therapy," *Journal of Family Psychotherapy* 21, no. 2 (2010): 117–131, doi:10.1080/08975350902967333.

6. Ibid., 125.

7. Ibid., 129.

CHAPTER 2

1. Jessica E. Donn and Richard C. Sherman, "Attitudes and Practices Regarding the Formation of Romantic Relationships on the Internet," *CyberPsychology & Behavior* 5, no. 2 (2004): 107–123. doi:10.1089/109493102753770499.

2. Nancy Baym, *Personal Connections in the Digital Age* (Malden, MA: Polity Press, 2010): 100.

3. Andrea Baker, "Down the Rabbit Hole: The Role of Place in the Initiation and Development of Online Relationships," 2008, quoted in Nancy Baym, *Personal Connections in the Digital Age* (Malden, MA: Polity Press, 2010): 126.

4. Baym, *Personal Connections*, 164.

5. Kiley A. Larson, "Negotiating Romantic and Sexual Relationships: Patterns and Meanings of Mediated Interaction" (PhD diss., University of Kansas, 2010): 128, https://kuscholarworks.ku.edu/bitstream/handle/1808/7828/larson_ku_0099d_11535_data_1.pdf?sequence=1.

6. Baym, *Personal Connections*, 164.

7. Amanda Klein, "Text Messaging: Effects on Romantic Relationships and Social Behavior," *Huffington Post*, August 22, 2012, http://www.huffingtonpost.com/amanda-klein/texting-romantic-relationships_b_1821646.html.

8. Susan Weinschenk, "Shopping, Dopamine, and Anticipation," *Psychology Today*, October 22, 2015, https://www.psychologytoday.com/blog/brain-wise/201510/shopping-dopamine-and-anticipation.

9. David Dobbs, "Sapolsky on Dopamine: Not About Pleasure, But Its Anticipation," *Wired* online, July 29, 2011, https://www.wired.com/2011/07/sapolsky-on-dopamine-not-about-pleasure-but-its-anticipation/.

10. Helen Fisher, *The Brain in Love*, TED Talk video, February 2008, https://www.ted.com/talks/helen_fisher_studies_the_brain_in_love.

11. Neil Strauss, *Rules of the Game* (New York: HarperCollins Publishers, 2007): 13.

12. Gregory L. Jantz, "Brain Differences between Genders," *Psychology Today*, February 27, 2014, 5, https://www.psychologytoday.com/blog/hope-relationships/201402/brain-differences-between-genders.

13. Robert Heasley, "Queer Masculinities of Straight Men," *Men and Masculinities* 7, no. 3 (2005): 310–320, doi:10.1177/1097184X04272118.

14. Aziz Ansari and Eric Klinenberg, *Modern Romance* (New York: Penguin Press, 2016): 64.

15. Erin R. Whitchurch, Timothy D. Wilson, and Daniel T. Gilbert, "He Loves Me, He Loves Me Not . . .: Uncertainty Can Increase Romantic Attraction," *Psychological Science* 22, no. 2 (2011): 172–175, doi:10.1177/0956797610393745.

16. Ansari, *Modern Romance*, 63.

17. Cindy Hazan and Phillip Shaver, "Romantic Love Conceptualized as an Attachment Process," *Journal of Personality and Social Psychology* 52, no. 3 (1987): 511–524, doi:10.1037/0022-3514.52.3.511.

18. Robert Weisskirch and Raquel Delevi, " 'Sexting' and Adult Romantic Attachment," *Computers in Human Behavior* 27, no. 5 (2011): 1697–1701, doi:10.1016/j.chb.2011.02.008.

CHAPTER 3

1. Aaron Smith, "U.S. Smartphone Use in 2015," Pew Research Center, April 1, 2015, http://www.pewinternet.org/2015/04/01/us-smartphone-use-in-2015/.

2. Ellie Lisitsa, "The Sound Relationship House: Build Love Maps," The Gottman Institute (blog), November 7, 2012, https://www.gottman.com/blog/the-sound-relationship-house-build-love-maps/.

3. Christopher M. Barnes, Klodiana Lanaj, and Russell Johnson, "Research: Using a Smartphone after 9 pm Leaves Workers Disengaged," *Harvard Business Review* online, January 15, 2014, https://hbr.org/2014/01/research-using-a-smartphone-after-9-pm-leaves-workers-disengaged.

4. Andrew Lepp et al., "Exploring the Relationships between College Students' Cell Phone Use, Personality and Leisure," *Computers in Human Behavior* 43 (February 2015): 210–219, doi:10.1016/j.chb.2014.11.006.

5. Sherry Turkle, "Stop Googling. Let's Talk," *The New York Times* online, September 26, 2015, https://www.nytimes.com/2015/09/27/opinion/sunday/stop-googling-lets-talk .html.

6. Turkle, "Stop Googling," 2015.

7. Timothy Wilson et al., "Just Think: The Challenges of the Disengaged Mind," *Science* 345 (July 2014): 75–77. doi:10.1126/science.1250830.

8. "Digital Distraction," last modified May 30, 2017, http://www.digitalresponsibility .org/digital-distraction/.

9. Daniel J. Kruger, "What's Behind Phantom Cellphone Buzzes?" *The Conversation*, January 2016, https://theconversation.com/whats-behind-phantom-cellphone-buzzes-73829.

10. Randi Smith, "'Phantom Vibration Syndrome' Common in Cellphone Users," *CBS News*, January 12, 2016, http://www.cbsnews.com/news/phantom-vibration-syndrome-common-in-cellphone-users/.

11. Aaron Smith, "Cell Phone Attachment and Etiquette," *The Best (and Worst) of Mobile Connectivity*, Pew Research Center, November 30, 2012, http://www.pewinternet .org/2012/11/30/part-iv-cell-phone-attachment-and-etiquette/.

12. Jose De-Sola Gutierrez, Fernando Rodriquez de Fonseca, and Gabriel Rubio, "Cell-Phone Addiction: A Review," *Frontiers in Psychiatry* 7 (October 2016): 175, doi:10.3389/fpsyt.2016.00175.

13. "Signs and Symptoms of Cell Phone Addiction," PsychGuides.com, accessed on May 30, 2017, http://www.psychguides.com/guides/signs-and-symptoms-of-cell-phone-addiction/.

14. David Greenfield, *Virtual Addiction* (Oakland, CA: New Harbinger Publications, 1999).

15. David Greenfield, "Internet Abuse Test," The Center for Internet and Technology Addiction, accessed May 30, 2017, http://virtual-addiction.com/internet-abuse-test/. Used by permission of David Greenfield.

16. Sherry Turkle, *Reclaiming Conversation: The Power of Talk in a Digital Age* (New York: Penguin Press, 2015).

17. Jonathan Franzen, "Sherry Turkle's 'Reclaiming Conversation,'" *The New York Times*, September 28, 2015, https://www.nytimes.com/2015/10/04/books/review/jonathan-franzen-reviews-sherry-turkle-reclaiming-conversation.html.

18. T. Field, "Postpartum Depression Effects on Early Interactions, Parenting, and Safety Practices: A Review," *Infant Behavior & Development* 33, no. 1 (February 2010): 1–6, doi:10.1016/j.infbeh.2009.10.005.

19. Laura K. Guerrero and Kory Floyd, *Nonverbal Communication in Close Relationships* (Mahwah, NJ: Routledge, 2005), VII.

20. Ibid., 2.

21. Ibid.

22. J. Billieux et al., "Is Dysfunctional Use of the Mobile Phone a Behavioural Addiction? Confronting Symptom-Based versus Process-Based Approaches," *Clinical Psychology and Psychotherapy* 5 (September–October 2015): 460–480. doi:10.1002/cpp.1910. Used by permission of John Wiley and Sons via Copyright Clearance Center.

23. Jeffrey Hall, Nancy Baym, and Kate Miltner, "Put Down That Phone and Talk to Me: Understanding the Roles of Mobile Phone Norm Adherence and Similarity in Relationships," *Mobile Media & Communication* 2, no. 2 (April 2014): 134–153, doi:10.1177/2050 157913517684.

CHAPTER 4

1. Hayley Krischer, "Can Jealousy Be Good for a Relationship?" *CNN* online, October 3, 2014, http://www.cnn.com/2014/02/18/living/jealousy-healthy-relationship-upwave/index.html.

2. Katherine M. Hertlein and Armeda Stevenson, "The Seven 'As' Contributing to Internet-Related Intimacy Problems: A Literature Review," *Cyberpsychology* 4, no. 1 (2010): article 3, https://cyberpsychology.eu/article/view/4230/3273.

3. Katherine M. Hertlein and Katrina Ancheta, "Advantages and Disadvantages of Technology in Relationships: Findings from an Open-Ended Survey," *The Qualitative Report* 19, no. 11 (2014): 1–11, http://nsuworks.nova.edu/tqr/vol19/iss11/2.

4. Ellen J. Helsper and Monica T. Whitty, "Netiquette within Married Couples: Agreement about Acceptable Online Behavior and Surveillance between Partners," *Computers in Human Behavior* 26, no. 5 (2010): 916–926. doi:10.1016/j.chb.2010.02.006.

5. Marlene Wasserman, *Cyber Infidelity: The New Seduction* (Cape Town, South Africa: Human & Rousseau, 2015).

6. Marlene Wasserman, interview by Rachel L. Hoffman, December 2016.

7. Ibid.

8. "AASECT Position on Sex Addiction," AASECT website, accessed on June 10, 2017, https://www.aasect.org/position-sex-addiction. Used by permission of AASECT.

9. Amanda Maddox, Galena Rhoades, and Howard Markman, "Viewing Sexually-Explicit Materials Alone or Together: Associations with Relationship Quality," *Archives of Sexual Behavior* 40, no. 2 (2009): 441–448, doi:10.1007/s10508-009-9585-4.

10. Marley Resch and Kevin Alderson, "Female Partners of Men Who Use Pornography: Are Honesty and Mutual Use Associated with Relationship Satisfaction?" *Journal of Sex and Marital Therapy* 40, no. 5 (2013): 410–424, doi:10.1080/0092623X.2012.751077.

11. Marty Klein, *His Porn, Her Pain* (Santa Barbara, CA: Praeger, 2016).

12. "Pornhub's 2016 Year in Review," *Pornhub Insights*, January 4, 2017, https://www.pornhub.com/insights/2016-year-in-review.

CHAPTER 5

1. Hui-Tzu Grace Chou and Nicholas Edge, "'They Are Happier and Having Better Lives Than I Am': The Impact of Using Facebook on Perceptions of Others' Lives," *Cyberpsychology, Behavior, and Social Networking* 15, no. 2 (February 2012): 117–121. doi:10.1089/cyber.2011.0324.

2. Ibid., 119.

3. Meredith Engel, "Why Do All Your Coupled-Up Friends Post Mushy Facebook Statuses," *New York Daily News*, August 12, 2014, http://www.nydailynews.com/life-style/coupled-folk-mushy-facebook-posts-article-1.1902392.

4. Sonja Utz and Camiel Beukeboom, "The Role of Social Network Sites in Romantic Relationships: Effects on Jealousy and Relationship Happiness," *Journal of Computer-Mediated Communication*, 16, no. 4 (July 2011): 511–527, doi:10.1111/j.1083–6101.2011.01552.x.

5. Amy Muise, Emily Christofides, and Serge Desmarais, "More Information Than You Ever Wanted: Does Facebook Bring Out the Green-Eyed Monster of Jealousy?" *Cyberpsychology & Behavior: The Impact of the Internet, Multimedia and Virtual Reality on Behavior and Society* 12, no. 4 (May 2009): 441–444, doi:10.1089/cpb.2008.0263.

6. Ibid., 442.

7. Rianne C. Farrugia, "Facebook and Relationships: A Study of How Social Media Use Is Affecting Long-Term Relationships" (PhD diss, Rochester Institute of Techology, 2013), 32, http://scholarworks.rit.edu/cgi/viewcontent.cgi?article=1033&context=theses.

8. Ibid. 33.

9. Rachel A. Elphinston and Patricia Noller, "Time to Face It! Facebook Intrusion and the Implications for Romantic Jealousy and Relationship Satisfaction," *Cyberpsychology, Behavior, and Social Networking* 14, no. 11 (May 2011): 631–635, doi:10.1089/cyber.2010.0318. Used by permission of Mary Ann Liebert, Inc. via Copyright Clearance Center.

CHAPTER 6

1. Aaron Smith, "15% of American Adults Have Used Online Dating Sites or Mobile Dating Apps," Pew Research Center, February 11, 2016, http://www.pewinternet.org/2016/02/11/15-percent-of-american-adults-have-used-online-dating-sites-or-mobile-dating-apps/.

2. Trent A. Petrie and Jessica L. Strübel, "Love Me Tinder: Objectification and Psychosocial Well-Being," poster presented at the American Psychological Association Convention, Denver, CO, August 2016.

3. Ibid., 2016.

CHAPTER 7

1. Josey Vogels, "Textual Gratification: Quill or Keypad, It's All about Sex," *The Globe and Mail*, May 3, 2004, http://www.theglobeandmail.com/technology/textual-gratification-quill-or-keypad-its-all-about-sex/article1136823/.

2. Eli Rosenberg, "In Weiner's Wake, a Brief History of the Word 'Sexting,'" *The Atlantic*, June 9, 2011, https://www.theatlantic.com/national/archive/2011/06/brief-history-sexting/351598/.

3. "Sexting: What Parents Need to Know," KidsHealth.org, accessed on June 6, 2017, http://kidshealth.org/en/parents/2011-sexting.html.

4. Mark Theoharis, "Teen Sexting," NOLO, accessed on June 6, 2017, http://www.criminaldefenselawyer.com/crime-penalties/juvenile/sexting.htm

5. Kimberly Young, "Cybersex and Infidelity Online: Implications for Evaluation and Treatment," *Sexual Addiction and Compulsivity* 7, no. 10 (2000): 59–74, http://netaddiction.com/articles/cyberaffairs.pdf.

6. Shirley Glass, *Not Just Friends: Rebuilding Trust and Recovering Your Sanity after Infidelity* (New York: Free Press, 2007).

7. Ibid., 25.

8. Diane Kholos Wysocki and Cheryl Childers, "Let My Fingers Do the Talking: Sexting and Infidelity in Cyberspace," *Sexuality & Culture* 15, no. 3 (September 2011): 217–239, doi:10.1007/s12119-011-9091-4.

9. Monica Whitty, "Pushing the Wrong Buttons: Men's and Women's Attitudes toward Online and Offline Infidelity," *Cyberpsychology Behavior* 6, no. 6 (December 2003): 569–579, doi:10.1089/109493103322725342.

10. Ibid., 65.

11. Michael Salter, "Privates in the Online Public: Sex(ting) and Reputation on Social Media," *New Media & Society* 18, no. 11 (2016): 2723–2739, doi:10.1177/1461444815604133.

12. Ibid., 2730.

13. Gary Chapman, *The 5 Love Languages: The Secret to Love That Lasts* (Chicago, IL: Northfield Publishing, 2014).

14. Rebecca Klein, *Frequently Asked Questions about Texting, Sexting, and Flaming* (New York: Rosen Classroom, 2012).

CHAPTER 8

1. L. Crystal Jiang and Jeffrey T. Hancock, "Absence Makes the Communication Grow Fonder: Geographic Separation, Interpersonal Media, and Intimacy in Dating Relationships," *Journal of Communication* 63, no. 3 (2013): 556–577, doi:10.1111/jcom.12029.

2. Emma Dargie et al., "Go Long! Predictors of Positive Relationship Outcomes in Long-Distance Dating Relationships," *Journal of Sex & Marital Therapy* 41 (March 2014): 181–202, doi:10.1080/0092623X.2013.864367.

3. Jiang, "Absence Makes the Communication," 557.

4. Ibid.

5. Ibid.

6. Marianne Dainton and Brooks Aylor, "Patterns of Communication Channel Use in the Maintenance of Long-Distance Relationships," *Communication Research Reports* 19, no. 2 (2002): 118–129, doi:10.1080/08824090209384839.

7. Rachelle Delva et al., "Satisfaction and the Use of Social Media in Geographically Distant Relationships," *Meta-Communicate* 3, no. 2 (2013), http://journals.chapman.edu/ojs/index.php/mc/article/view/882.

8. Ibid., 15.

9. Byrony Cole, "About Future of Sex," Future of Sex podcast site, accessed June 10, 2017, http://www.futureofsex.org/.

10. Jiang, "Absence Makes the Communication," 556.

11. "Latest Telecommuting Statistics," Global Workplace Analytics, updated January 2016, http://globalworkplaceanalytics.com/telecommuting-statistics2016.

12. Carman Neustadter, founder of the Connections Lab, interviewed by Rachel Hoffman, March 29, 2017.

CHAPTER 9

1. Andrew Hess, "3 Ways Dating Has Changed in the Last 20 Years," ChristianMingle.com, December 16, 2016, https://www.christianmingle.com/believe/3-ways-dating-has-changed/#6LVbttspMlGrqOwb.97.

2. Barry Schwartz, *The Paradox of Choice: Why More Is Less* (New York: HarperCollins Publishers, 2009).

3. Barry Schwartz, "More Isn't Always Better," *Harvard Business Review* online, June 2006, https://hbr.org/2006/06/more-isnt-always-better.

4. Aziz Ansari and Eric Klinenberg, *Modern Romance* (New York: Penguin Press, 2016).

5. Aziz Ansari, "Everything You Thought You Knew about L-O-V-E Is Wrong," *Time* online, October 10, 2015, http://time.com/aziz-ansari-modern-romance/.

6. David Yarus, founder of JSwipe, interviewed by Rachel Hoffman, December 27, 2016.

7. Brian Dunham, founder of OhMiBod, interviewed by Rachel Hoffman, February 28, 2017.

8. Brené Brown, *Daring Greatly: How the Courage to Be Vulnerable Transforms the Way We Live, Love, Parent and Lead* (London: Penguin UK, 2013): 249.

9. "Millennials in Adulthood: Detached from Institutions, Networked with Friends," Pew Research Center online, March 7, 2014, http://www.pewsocialtrends.org/2014/03/07/millennials-in-adulthood/.

10. Aaron Smith, "15% of American Adults Have Used Online Dating Sites or Mobile Dating Apps," Pew Research Center, February 11, 2016, http://www.pewinternet.org/2016/02/11/15-percent-of-american-adults-have-used-online-dating-sites-or-mobile-dating-apps/.

11. Helen Fisher, *Technology Hasn't Changed Love. Here's Why*, TED Talk video, June 2016, https://www.ted.com/talks/helen_fisher_technology_hasn_t_changed_love_here_s_why.

12. Jean Twenge, R.A. Sherman, and B.E. Wells, "Changes in American Adults' Sexual Behavior and Attitudes, 1972–2012," *Archives of Sexual Behavior* 44, no. 8 (November 2015): 2273–2285, doi:10.1007/s10508–015–0540–2.

13. Elizabeth Landau, "Commitment for Millennials: Is It Okay, Cupid?" *Scientific American* (blog), February 8, 2017, https://blogs.scientificamerican.com/mind-guest-blog/commitment-for-millennials-is-it-okay-cupid/.

14. Nancy Jo Sales, "Tinder and the Dawn of the 'Dating Apocalypse,'" *Vanity Fair* online, September 2015, http://www.vanityfair.com/culture/2015/08/tinder-hook-up-culture-end-of-dating.

15. "Introducing the New Hinge," Hinge homepage, accessed June 7, 2017, https://thedatingapocalypse.com/.

16. Jared Weiss, founder of Touchpoint, interviewed by Rachel Hoffman, January 13, 2017.

17. Ibid.

18. Daniel Mochon, "Single Option Aversion," *Journal of Consumer Research* 40, no. 3 (October 2013): 555–566, doi:10.1086/671343.

19. Mochon, "Single Option Aversion," 555.

CHAPTER 10

1. Sarah Louise Ryan, "7 Truths about Ghosting in a Breakup You Probably Didn't Know," *Sarah Louise Ryan* (blog), March 20, 2016, https://www.sarahlouiseryan.com/single-post/2016/03/20/7-Truths-About-Ghosting-In-A-Breakup-You-Probably-Didnt-Know.

2. Almas Nazir, psychiatrist, interviewed by Rachel Hoffman, March 28, 2017.

3. Nora Crotty, "Generation Ghost: The Facts behind the Slow Fade," *Elle* online, July 11, 2014, http://www.elle.com/life-love/sex-relationships/advice/a12787/girls-ghosting-relationships/.

4. Abraham Maslow, "A Theory of Human Motivation," *Psychological Review* 50 (1943): 370–396.

5. Valeriya Safronova, "Exes Explain Ghosting, the Ultimate Silent Treatment," *The New York Times* online, June 26, 2015, https://www.nytimes.com/2015/06/26/fashion/exes-explain-ghosting-the-ultimate-silent-treatment.html?_r=0.

6. Jessica Samakow, " 'Ghosting:' The 21st-Century Dating Problem Everyone Talks about, But No One Knows How to Deal With," *Huffington Post*, last updated October 31, 2014, http://www.huffingtonpost.com/2014/10/30/ghosting-dating-_n_6028958.html.

7. Karley Sciortino, "Breathless: To Ghost or Not to Ghost?" *Vogue* online, December 11, 2015, http://www.vogue.com/article/breathless-karley-sciortino-ghosting.

8. Roisin Lanigan, " 'Cushioning' Is the New Ghosting. Welcome to the Dating Trend You Don't Even Know You're Doing," Babe.com, February 7, 2017, http://thetab.com/uk/2017/02/07/cushioning-new-ghosting-welcome-dating-trend-dont-even-know-youre-32185.

9. Bela Gandhi, "Are You Being Cushioned? 5 Ways to Know," Today.com, April 21, 2017, http://www.today.com/health/are-you-being-cushioned-5-ways-know-t110631.

10. Jen Kim, "The Strange Psychology of Ghosting," *Psychology Today*, July 29, 2015, https://www.psychologytoday.com/blog/valley-girl-brain/201507/the-strange-psychology-ghosting.

CHAPTER 11

1. "The Common Sense Census: Plugged-In Parents of Tweens and Teens 2016," Common Sense Media, accessed June 8, 2017, https://www.commonsensemedia.org/research/the-common-sense-census-plugged-in-parents-of-tweens-and-teens-2016#.

2. Mari Swingle, *i-Minds: How Cell Phones, Computers, Gaming, and Social Media Are Changing Our Brains, Our Behavior, and the Evolution of Our Species* (British Columbia, Canada: New Society Publishers, 2016): 38.

3. Ibid., 40.

4. Katherine Hobson, "No Snapchat in the Bedroom? An Online Tool to Manage Kids' Media Use," *All Things Considered*, October 21, 2016, http://www.npr.org/sections/health-shots/2016/10/21/498706789/no-snapchat-in-the-bedroom-an-online-tool-to-manage-kids-media-use.

5. Georgene Troseth, associate professor of psychology at Vanderbilt University, interviewed by Katherine Hobson, *All Things Considered*, NPR, October 2016.

6. Dr. Almas Nazir, psychiatrist, interviewed by Rachel Hoffman, March 28, 2017.

ADDENDUM/LESSON PLAN

1. Lee Rainie and Kathryn Zickuhr, "Phone Use in Social Gatherings," *Americans' Views on Mobile Etiquette*, Pew Research Center online, August 26, 2015, http://www.pewinternet.org/2015/08/26/chapter-4-phone-use-in-social-gatherings/.

2. Sherry Turkle, *Alone Together: Why We Expect More from Technology and Less from Each Other* (Cambridge, MA: Perseus Books, 2013).

3. Sherry Turkle, "Stop Googling. Let's Talk," *The New York Times* online, September 26, 2015, https://www.nytimes.com/2015/09/27/opinion/sunday/stop-googling-lets-talk.html.

4. Cristina Jenaro et al., "Problematic Internet and Cell-Phone Use: Psychological, Behavioral, and Health Correlates," *Addiction Research & Theory* 15, no. 3 (July 2009): 309–320, doi:10.1080/16066350701350247.

5. Rainie and Zickuhr, "Phone Use in Social Gatherings," 2015.

INDEX

About the Author

RACHEL HOFFMAN, LCSW, is a therapist at the Long Island Institute of Sex Therapy. She is earning her doctoral degree in human sexuality from Widener University, Chester, Philadelphia. She is a member of both National Association of Social Workers (NASW) and American Association of Sexuality Educators, Counselors, and Therapists (AASECT). She is founder of the website RachelHoffman.org, which highlights her therapy practice and various companies in the sex and tech world. Her therapy website is sextherapylongisland.com.

About the Series Editor

JUDY KURIANSKY, Ph.D., is a licensed clinical psychologist and adjunct faculty in the Department of Clinical Psychology at Columbia University Teachers College and the Department of Psychiatry at Columbia University College of Physicians and Surgeons, as well as a visiting professor at Peking University Health Sciences Center and honorary professor in the Department of Psychiatry of the University of Hong Kong. A diplomate of the American Board of Sexology and fellow of the American Academy of Clinical Sexology, she was awarded the AACS Medal of Sexology for Lifetime Achievement. Dr. Judy is a pioneer of sex diagnosis, dating back to being on the DSM III committee; sex therapy evaluation, including of early Masters and Johnson therapy; and call-in advice about sex on the radio and TV. A cofounder of the Society for Sex Therapy and Research, and past board member of the American Association of Sex Educators, Counselors and Therapists (AASECT), she has authored hundreds of articles in professional journals, including the *Journal of Marital and Sex Therapy* and SIECUS reports, and mass market articles including in *Cosmopolitan* and *Family Circle* magazines. She has written sex advice columns worldwide, including for the *South China Morning Post*, *Singapore Straits Times*, *Sankei Sinbun* newspaper, and the *New York Daily News*. She has developed and led hundreds of workshops about sexuality around the world from China and Japan to India, Israel, Iran, Austria, and Argentina, including on an integration of Eastern and Western techniques for safe sex and for relationship enhancement.

Lightning Source UK Ltd.
Milton Keynes UK
UKHW022336021218
333339UK00004B/42/P